David Bachman Landis

The Landis Family of Lancaster County

A Comprehensive History of the Landis Folk...

David Bachman Landis

The Landis Family of Lancaster County
A Comprehensive History of the Landis Folk...

ISBN/EAN: 9783337210328

Printed in Europe, USA, Canada, Australia, Japan

Cover: Foto ©ninafisch / pixelio.de

More available books at **www.hansebooks.com**

THE

LANDIS FAMILY OF LANCASTER COUNTY,

—A—

COMPREHENSIVE HISTORY OF THE LANDIS FOLK

FROM THE

MARTYRS' ERA TO THE ARRIVAL OF THE
FIRST SWISS SETTLERS,

GIVING

THEIR NUMEROUS LINEAL DESCENDANTS;

ALSO, AN

*ACCURATE RECORD OF MEMBERS
IN THE REBELLION,*

WITH

A SKETCH OF THE START AND SUBSEQUENT GROWTH OF
LANDISVILLE AND LANDIS VALLEY,

AND

*A COMPLETE DIRECTORY OF LIVING
LANDIS ADULTS,*

ETC., ETC.

By D. B. LANDIS,
Ex-Editor of the Landisville Vigil.

"Non Nobis Solum."

LANCASTER, PA.
PUBLISHED AND PRINTED BY THE AUTHOR.
1888.

Press' of
THE WEEKLY INQUIRER,
Lancastor, Pa.

Bindery of
HALLOWELL & WEST,
Philadelphia.

TO THE

MEMORY

OF THAT

STURDY SWISS SETTLER,

➤ Benjamin Landis, ⭠

HIS BROTHERS,

AND

Benjamin Landis, Jr.,

FROM WHOM HAVE HONORABLY SPRUNG
THAT VAST RELATIONSHIP
KNOWN AS

The Landis Family of Lancaster County,

THESE HISTORICAL FACTS ARE RE-
SPECTFULLY INSCRIBED
BY

THE AUTHOR.

"From our Ancestors come our Names,
But from our Virtues our Honors."

PREFATORY.

JUST ten short months since, while the writer's mind during some leisure moments was diverted to the genealogy of his family forefathers, he became suddenly convinced that a history of the stock, embracing all persons in this county bearing the name of Landis, was a necessity. He, therefore, at once undertook the voluntary task of compiling this work, with no other material at hand than a little information concerning his immediate family predecessors.

Had it not been for a host of friends, both old and new, who aided by tongue and pen, this little volume could not have been issued in the specified time; especially since it was prepared amid the manifold interruptions incident to a busy typographer's life. The author acknowledges his particular obligations to: Rev. John L. Landis, Binkley's Bridge; Rev. John B. Landis, East Petersburg; Levi S. Reist, Oregon; Hon. John H. Landis, Millersville; M. B. Landis, Washington, D. C.; Israel C. Landis, Landisville; Prof. F. W. Bushong, Wichita, Kansas; John F. Landis, Elizabethtown; A. G. Landis, Sterling, Kan.; Jacob F. Landis, Abilene, Kan.; Eli B. Landis, Philadelphia; Henry H. Landis, Landis Valley; James D. Landis, Lancaster; M. R. Landis, Richland, Lebanon county; Ezra F. Landis, Lancaster; D. K. Landis, Strasburg; Martin G. Landis, East Lampeter; Benjamin K. Landis, Bird-in-Hand; Emma Lehman, Landisville; and a number of others, for valuable aid in obtaining information from their respective families or localities. Among the publications from which extracts have been made, are: *Martyrs' Mirror*, *Rupp's History of Lancaster County*, *Harris' Biographical History of Lancaster County*, *Evans' History of Lancaster County*, the Lancaster *Inquirer*, *New Era*, and Landisville *Vigil*.

It has been the writer's desire to give a useful compendium of local knowledge that will benefit others besides those of his name. In addition to two parts of genealogy, a complete record of Landis soldiers is appended; also, an original account of the progress of Landisville and Landis Valley; a directory of living adults; and general information. A brief biography, in plain language, is given of each individual; also, the exact generation of every family from the earliest inhabitants. Nick-names are introduced throughout these pages more for the purpose of distinguishing similarity of surnames than to show their oddity.

Should the reception of this volume, with its necessarily limited first edition, prove favorable, a second volume may follow. In the meantime the present book can be had for 65 cents cash, or the illustrated autograph edition for $1.25.

D. B. L.

320 E. Chestnut St., Lancaster, Pa.,
February 1, 1888.

CONTENTS.

PART I.

ANCESTRY AND EARLY SETTLERS.

PART II.

GROWTH OF THE LANDIS FAMILY.

PART III.

LANDIS SOLDIERS OF THE REBELLION.

PART IV.

LANDISVILLE AND LANDIS VALLEY.

THE
Landis Family of Lancaster County.

PART I.

ANCESTRY AND EARLY SETTLERS.

PERSECUTIONS OF MENNONITES IN THE SEVENTEENTH CEN-
TURY—MIGRATION OF LANDISES TO AMERICA—FIRST SET-
TLERS IN THE CONESTOGA VALLEY—LINEAL DESCENDANTS
OF THE EIGHTEENTH CENTURY.

IN the latter part of the Sixteenth century the Landises,
among others in Switzerland, were noted for their piety,
and were appropriately called Pietists. The first historical mention of individual members of the Landis family is
made of Hans Landis,* a "pious witness of the Divine truth,"
who existed at that time. Hans was a Pietus or Mennonite
preacher, who moved to the Rhine, in Switzerland, and lived
there to feed and refresh others who were seeking after right-
eousness. The Council of Zurich, who be it known were not
Catholics, but of the Reformed† church, ordered Hans' arrest,
thus thinking to stop his teachings. But that good man could

---

* "Martyrs' Mirror," translated by Rupp, 1837; p. 1003.
† After the fearful persecutions of Protestants by Catholics during the
Sixteenth century, some of the *Reformed* placed themselves on record at
Zurich and Berne as continuators of the cruel practices known to the
martyrs' era. Various edicts were issued from 1601 to 1660 by the Reformed against the Anabaptists (derisive of Baptists or Mennonites),
creating fines, confiscation of property and other stringent penalties, including banishment. Others, however, of the Reformed belief, especially the regents of the United Netherlands, exerted their influence for
the protection of the innocent Mennonites.

not be deterred from his sincere convictions, and "he was taken prisoner by his enemies and sent in irons from Zurich to the papists at Zolothurn." After being liberated by the aid of some kind-natured persons, he was again retaken and sent to Zurich, where he was rigorously examined as to his doctrine. In September, 1614, he was beheaded* with a sword, as a true follower of Christ. The authorities then tried to persuade the common people that Hans was decapitated for his obstinacy towards them, but it remains a fact that he suffered death for religion's sake.

It is interesting to know that Hans Landis was the last person to be beheaded for religious convictions in that locality, but persecution did not cease with his death. In May, 1637, among three other brethren, "Hans Landis, the second, a steadfast minister of the church in Horgerberg, and his daughter, Margaretha," were confined full sixty weeks at Othenbach. "Meantime the authorities sold their property for 7000 florins, and applied it to their own use."†

In 1640, "Oswald Landis, his wife, and two daughters-in-law, were incarcerated in Othenbach. Jacob Landis, Oswald's son, and all his family, were banished. The two daughters-in-law, with their infants, escaped from prison; which good fortune afterwards befell the old man and his wife. But they had to forsake all their property, and wander about in poverty."‡

Felix Landis (son of Hans, beheaded at Zurich, 1614) was

---

*The following extract from a letter dated July 19-29, 1659, written by a preacher at Zurich, gives an accurate description of the execution: "Hans Landis was tall of stature, had a long black beard, a little gray, and a masculine voice. Being led out cheerfully with a rope, to Wolfsstatt, the place of decollation, the executioner, Mr. Paul Volmar, let the rope fall [not, however, before Hans' wife and child came to him with tears in their eyes to bid him a last farewell, after which he entreated them to depart so as not to shake his resolution to meet his fate], raised both hands to heaven, and said: 'O, God of mercy, to thee be it complained, that you, Hans, have fallen into my hands; for God's sake forgive me for what I must do to you,' etc. Hans consoled the executioner, saying: 'I have already forgiven you, may God forgive you also; I am aware that you must execute the sentence of the magistracy; be undismayed, and see that nothing hinders you in this matter,' etc., whereupon he was beheaded."

† Martyrs' Mirror, p. 1009.

‡ Martyrs' Mirror, p. 1016.

a pious member of the church of Horgerberg. For this he was committed to Othenbach, and treated with shameful rigor, often receiving no food. His digestive organs became so impaired through protracted fasting, that his stomach refused to retain food, and he accordingly prepared himself for death. In this state he was carried by the persecutors to church during the sermon, where he was brutally "thrown under a bench," and when he immediately expired. "His wife, Adelheyd Egli, was also kept in durance in Othenbach nearly four years. During this period they treated her not only unmercifully, but disgracefully; they threw her into several offensive places, stripped her twice in irons, and for a time took her clothes from her every night, etc."* She escaped afterward from prison with a good conscience. Meantime the authorities ruthlessly dispersed her family, drove the children among strangers, and then confiscated her house and furniture and sold them for 5000 florins.

One night in 1643, the beadles attacked the house of Verena Landis, an elderly sister. They made such a tumult that Verena became faint and sick and could not go with the servitors of the authorities. She was thereupon compelled to "promise that she would remain a prisoner in her own house, which promise she accordingly fulfilled."† As she was harshly treated and supplied with poor provisions, death soon resulted.

About 1660, and afterward, the Landises were driven to the Palatinate country, to Zweiburg and Alsace, neighborhood of Strasburg and Manheim on the Rhine. Their properties were generally confiscated; and they became farmers for the German nobility. All the Mennonites received fair usage from the Hollanders and people of the United Netherlands.

MIGRATING TO AMERICA.

For about two generations history fails to reveal individual members of the Landis family, *i. e.* from 1643 to 1717. Members of the Mennonite belief early took advantage of William Penn's liberal policy to settle in America. About 1683, and

---

* Martyrs' Mirror, p. 1017.
† Martyrs' Mirror, p. 1018.

later in 1709 and 1712, numbers of them emigrated to Chester county (including what is now the county of Lancaster). In 1717, three brothers,* Rev. Benjamin,† Felix and John Landis, all Swiss Mennonites, came to America from the vicinity of Manheim on the Rhine, where they had been driven from Zurich, Switzerland, and purchased land from Penn and the Conestogoe Indians. Like most of the pioneer settlers in the American wilds, these good people were comparatively poor in worldly possessions, and had their hands so full of work that they failed, it seems, to keep their family records. They became, however, instinctively American in their progress, and proceeded at once to skillfully till the soil which has since made this county known the world over as a "garden spot." Here, also, these pioneer members of the family worshiped their God according to their desire, and in perfect peace.

Benjamin's lineal descendants being numerous and mostly located in the present confines of Lancaster county, his vast family obtains precedence throughout this volume; while the descendants of his two brothers, Felix and John (and others who emigrated afterward), are also given wherever they are connected with the history of this county.

BENJAMIN LANDIS, OF LANCASTER COUNTY.

Rev. Benjamin Landis,[1] one of the three brothers who emigrated to America, accompanied by an only son, Benjamin, jr. (aged 18), took up a tract of 240 acres of land from the London Company, for which he received a patent in 1718.‡ This land was in possession of the Conestogoe Indians, from whom it was obtained by purchase. Benjamin was a Mennonite preacher, and, with his son, began farming on his tract,§ situ-

---

* Descendants of those who were persecuted in the Seventeenth century.
† In Taylor's surveys of the old patent tracts, Jacob Landis is said to have taken out the patent for a tract; and in 1718 the first assessment made in Conestogoe township (now Lancaster county) included the names of Jacob Landis and Jacob Landis, jr. From the various records extant it seems as if the name of Jacob on the old surveys was a mistake, and that it was intended for Benjamin, who had also a son, Benjamin, jr.
‡ Evans' History of Lancaster County, 1883.
§ Most of the original tract is now owned by the Henry N. Landis family.

ated in what is now East Lampeter township, near Mellinger's meeting-house, about four miles east of Lancaster city, at the intersection of the Horse-shoe and old Philadelphia roads. No records tell to whom this pious man was married, and, unfortunately, for several succeeding generations, such information is very meagre.

Benjamin Landis, jr.,[2] the younger immigrant, had four sons, whose names in the order of their births* and respective ages were: Benjamin, Abraham, Jacob, and Henry. These four sons were the first born upon the soil, from whom have sprung the numerous descendants of Benjamin.[1] Little mention is made in any records obtainable of daughters, although such were born, without doubt, to some of the first generations. Benjamin, jr., tilled the soil of his father's farm and lived there.

Benjamin Landis,[3] oldest son of the younger immigrant, moved to Manheim township, in 1751–3, after buying his wife's only brother† out, which left him 800 or 1,000 acres of land‡ about three miles from Lancaster city, near the Reading road and close to where the Landis Valley meeting-house now stands. Benjamin was married, in 1749, to Anna Snavely, only daughter of John Snavely. They had three sons: Hansle (John),§ born March 15, 1755; Bennie (Benjamin), born in the winter of 1756; and Henry, born December 5, 1760. Benjamin's[3] place "was the refuge of many Swiss emigrants, who enjoyed his hospitality until they were able to secure homes for themselves."

Abraham Landis,[3] second son‖ of the younger immigrant, had two sons: Benjamin and John. Benjamin, the oldest,

---

*This method of naming children is adhered to wherever possible throughout this book.

†Mr. Snavely purchased 1,000 acres originally from John Herr and Martin [?] Landis about 1718.—*Lancaster New Era, December, 1885.*

‡Assessed in 1779, for 650 acres of land; 1786, 550 acres.—*From returns now in the Commissioners' office, Lancaster.*

§John was one among a number of non-associators of 1777, according to history. These persons were generally assessed the sum of £3, 10s., for the prosecution of the Revolutionary War, in which they refused to take part.

‖Assessed in 1756, for 150 acres of land.

lived in East Lampeter township; John, second son, called "Musser" John, also resided in East Lampeter.

Jacob Landis,[3] third son of the younger immigrant, had two sons and six daughters, viz.: Barbara (Weaver), Lizzie (Houser), John ("Brick"), born July 3, 1766; Abraham, born November 1, 1767; Esther (Burkholder), —— (Mrs. Jacob Groff), —— (Harnish), —— (Winters). Two of the latter were named Mary and Magdalena.* Jacob was Collector of Taxes "for the King's use" in East Lampeter township, in 1763. He died during the summer of 1794.

Henry Landis,[3] was the youngest son of Benjamin,[2] the younger immigrant. He had five sons: Benjamin, John, Henry, Peter, and Abraham. (See page 17.)

FELIX LANDIS, OF DAUPHIN COUNTY.

Felix Landis,[1] a brother of Rev. Benjamin, received a patent in 1719-20, from the London Company, for 400 acres of land on Mill Creek, near Witmer's Bridge (then known as Conestoga township,† now East Lampeter). Felix established a mill‡ on his tract. In 1731 he granted part of this property to John Binckle, as then written, who appears to have been a relative.§ It is said that the first generation of Felix sold out and removed to Dauphin and Lebanon counties (then known as Derry township, Lancaster county). His children were: Felix, jr.,|| Anna, Barbara, Froncka (married to Abra-

---

* From the recorded Will in Register's office, Lancaster.

† Felix was assessed in 1718—the first assessment made in Conestoga township.

‡ An old mill stood on this site until 1882, when it was sold by D. B. Landis (miller) to Isaac Groff, who erected a fine new brick mill in its place. The old corner-stone was preserved and placed in the corner of the new engine house.

§ John Binckley died intestate in 1760, leaving three sons: Felix, Henry and John. At the division of the property Felix Binckley took the water-right and land adjoining, consisting of 113 acres and 96 perches, and in 1767 built the mill at Millport. Felix died in this county and is supposed to be buried at Mellinger's graveyard, although no stone bearing his name can be found.—*Evans' History of Lancaster County.*

|| A public document having, among many others, the name of Felix Landis, jr., recorded in it, being an act passed *Anno Regni Georgii II. Regis Magnae Brittanniae, Franciae et Hiberniae, tertio*, October 14, 1729, gave authority to "the Hon. Patrick Gordon, esq., Lieutenant-Governor of the Province of Pennsylvania," etc., to have and enjoy the

ham Miers). His Will was recorded in 1739, being the first on record here of the Landis family. Felix, jr.'s Will, being written in High Dutch, was not recorded, but simply endorsed.

The third generation settled at Spring Creek, Dauphin county, the Landises there upholding the name of Felix for generations.

JOHN LANDIS, OF BUCKS COUNTY.

John Landis,[1] a brother of Rev. Benjamin, and a native of Switzerland, after arriving in America in 1717, located in Bucks county, this State. He had five sons, viz.: John, Jacob, Martin, George, and Samuel; and two daughters, Veronica and Barbara.[*]

John Landis,[2] one of the five sons, was born in Bucks county, November 11, 1720, and removed to Montgomery county, this State.

Jacob Landis[2] was born in Montgomery county, this State. He died in 1806, near Jersey Shore, Lycoming county, whence he had removed. His children were: Solomon, John, Joseph, Benjamin, Nancy, and Betsy. Their occupations were various, and they lived at divers places—John and Joseph removing to Lancaster county.

JOHN LANDIS, OF EPHRATA.

About the year 1720 John Landis[†] took up three or four hundred acres of land below the junction of Middle and Ham-mer Creeks running into the Cocalico, between what is now Akron and the Oil Works. He started a graveyard near Akron, where five generations of Landises are buried. He was the founder of most of the Ephrata stock.

The later descendants of Felix Landis, of Dauphin; John, of Bucks; and John, of Ephrata, are given at the close of Part II.; also, the genealogy of "Hill" John, and others.

"privileges and advantages of natural born subjects. as fully, to all in-tents and constructions and purposes, whatsoever, as any of his [King George's] natural born subjects," etc.

[*] From a sketch of the Landis Family, by Andrew M. Frantz, esq., in Harris' Biographical History of Lancaster County, 1872.

[†] By some folks claimed to be a brother of Rev. Benjamin, the first settler. There no doubt existed some relationship, but Benjamin's real brother John then was in Bucks county.

PART II.

GROWTH OF THE LANDIS FAMILY.

EMBRACING THE PERIOD FROM ABOUT THE REVOLUTIONARY
TIME TO THE PRESENT DAY—GENEALOGICAL SKETCHES,
WITH BIRTHS, MARRIAGES AND DEATHS OF MANY MEM-
BERS—A VARIETY OF OTHER INFORMATION.

SINCE the days when our forefathers experienced the trials incident to a separation from English rule, the spread of the Landis family has been remarkably rapid; and "there is no family so closely and so essentially connected with the growth and development of Lancaster county" as this one. As a family, too, it has been steadily devoted to farming through successive generations, who "are not so much distinguished for producing great public men as for the uniform private worth of all its members"—and yet some of them *have* shown their aptitude for other than agricultural pursuits. They have maintained, in a large degree, the genuine Lancaster county character, having been industrious and economical without almost an exception. This, together, with the natural modesty and coolness of the stock, has proved a safe shield against the allurements of speculation and excitements, and has kept the family largely together on its native farms.

GENEALOGICAL SKETCHES.

Beginning with the oldest branch of the original settler in Lancaster county, the genealogy of the Landis family is given on the following pages as complete as it could be procured. The numerous descendants of Rev. Benjamin[1] are given first, viz.:

LINEAL DESCENDANTS OF JOHN.[4]

(Continued from page 14.)

"So-zu-sauga"* John Landis,[4] so called from his frequent use of the words "so to say," lived in East Lampeter township, and was the oldest son of Benjamin.[3] He had three sons: John, Benjamin and Henry. He lived on his father's farm, and died in May, 1837, at the advanced age of 82 years.

"Swamp" John Landis[5] was born in Lampeter township, September 11, 1782. He went to Landisville on a farm, and married Anna Bachman, by whom he had three children who reached maturity: John C., Michael B. and Elizabeth. He started storekeeping at "Centreville" (now Landisville) in the spring of 1829, having purchased land from Jacob Charles in the fall of 1828. (See Part IV.) He was Landisville's first Postmaster, and remained a citizen of that place until his demise, April 16, 1863; aged 80 years, 7 months and 5 days. His wife, who was born February 3, 1785, died May 23, 1846; aged 61 years, 3 months and 20 days.

John C. Landis,[6] first son of John Landis,[5] of East Hempfield township, was born on August 31, 1807. His later school days were spent at John Beck's famous Academy for Boys, in Lititz, from about 1823 to 1825, when and where he acquired a thorough knowledge of mathematics, astronomy and surveying. He was an expert chirographer and reader in both English and German. After leaving school he followed surveying in Landisville, which village was laid out by him and his father in 1828–30. (See Part IV.) From 1829 to 1832 he was a salesman in his father's store. On January 5, 1832, he was united in marriage, by Rev. Lœffler, to Veronica (commonly called Fanny) Shelly. Four children resulted from this union: Ann Eliza, the first child, was born May 14, 1833. Israel Christian was the second by birth. Jacob was born April 23, 1841, and died September 4, 1845; aged 4 years, 4 months and 11 days. Albert Shelly, born August 20, 1847; died August 15, 1849, aged only 1 year, 11 months and 26 days. John C. was one of the originators of the Bethel church at Landisville, founded by John Winebrenner,

---

* He was also known by some persons as "Hansle."

and a consistent member thereof. He kept a general merchandise establishment from about 1833 in his native village,
and died March 25, 1854, from an apoplectic stroke received
while in his store; his age was 46 years, 6 months and 25
days. Fanny, his wife, lived, until her demise, west of where
Minnich's hotel is now located. She died at the age of 69
years and 25 days, on January 13, 1879.

Ann Eliza Landis[7] became the wife of Joseph G. Greider, a
farmer, of East Hempfield township. Her children, all living,
are: John, Joseph L. and Benjamin. She died a few days
previous to her mother, in 1879.

Israel Christian Landis[7] was born September 24, 1835. His
father was John C., of Landisville. Israel, after receiving a
common education, spent his last school days in James P.
Wickersham's Academy, Marietta. His father dying suddenly, he was thrown upon his own resources for a living.
He was married by Rev. W. T. Gerhard, January 17, 1861,
to Mary Musselman, after which he kept an oyster saloon in
Landisville for five years. During this time a son was born,
who was named David Bachman. A daughter called Florence
Shelly, was born April 6, 1865. Mr. Landis then removed to
Centreville, East Hempfield township, where farming occupied
his attention for two years. From there he went to Rohrerstown, where he kept a confectionery and lived three years.
He built a house on a tract of land 1½ miles west of the latter
place, whence he removed and lived one year. Hearing of an
opportunity to rent a store stand in Salunga, he sold his new
property and did a thriving trade in general merchandise for
three years, besides being Postmaster of the last-named village. In the fall of 1874 he built a new store near Bamford
Brothers' zinc mines, the place afterward being named Bamfordville.* Since then he has been engaged in business there.
In politics he has always been a Republican; and in business
a careful manager.

David Bachman Landis[8] is the only son of Israel C., and
was born in Landisville, February 12, 1862. He received a
common school education. Was a clerk in his father's store,
at Bamfordville, for some years. In March, 1877, during

---

* So named, in 1875, by the writer of this sketch.

school days, he first brought to light a small boys' paper, named the *Keystone Amateur*. In April of the following year it was first printed by him, under the title of the *Amateur, Jr.* In August of that year, the sheet was enlarged to a 16-page magazine, including covers, under the original name; and with the October number it ceased publication. On the 7th of October, 1878, David was apprenticed to the Inquirer Printing and Publishing Company, Lancaster, to learn Guttenberg's art. After serving four years at the trade, he opened a professional job printing office in Landisville, in April, 1883. On May 1 of the same year, he issued the initial number of the *Village Vigil*, as a tri-monthly; in a year it was printed weekly; and in 1885 the paper was enlarged to eight pages, being known thereafter as the Landisville *Vigil*. He has been a frequent contributor to the *Inquirer* and the *New Era*, of Lancaster; the *Wheel*,* New York; the *Wheelman* (magazine), Boston; and other journals. He was married to Nora K., daughter of David Baker, deceased, of East Hempfield township, on Tuesday, September 29, 1885, by Rev. Dr. E. Greenwald, late of Lancaster. September 19, 1886, a daughter, named Katie Musselman, was born. On March 13, 1886, the *Vigil* was discontinued, the owner connecting himself with the Lancaster *Inquirer*, in which establishment he has had charge of the printing since then.

Elizabeth Landis,[6] daughter of John Landis,[5] was born October 29, 1811. She was married by Rev. Lœffler, at Lititz, to John Lehman, September 29, 1829. She had six children: John, who died at the age of 6 years; Henry C., Lancaster; Annie (Martin); Mary A. (Swarr); Emma, and Adeline. Mrs. Lehman (widow) resides in Landisville.

Michael Bachman Landis,[6]† second son of John Landis, of East Hempfield township, was born in September, 1819. Was three months a student of John Beck's Lititz Academy; went to two select schools—one in Niagara county, N. Y., and the other at Williamsville, Erie county, N. Y.; attended

*As a pioneer cyclist he was thrice appointed Consul of Landisville, by the Pennsylvania Division of the League of American Wheelmen.

†M. B. L.'s grandfather on his mother's side, Michael Bachman, after whom he was named, died in the same year as his grandfather Landis, in 1837. Bachman's age was near 80.

Susquehanna Institute, Marietta, Pa., six months; also went to Joseph Dando's Institute for Accountants, in Philadelphia. He was married to Barbara Ziegler, of East Donegal township, in 1844. Solon, his son, was born in September, 1845. Michael B. taught school in Warwick township, this county; also, in Dauphin county, this State; California, Oregon and Iowa. Resided in Iowa from 1851 to 1863; in California and Oregon from 1868 to 1876. Was an employee in the United States Land Office at Fort Dodge, Iowa, for several years; a census enumerator in 1880 for part of Lancaster city, Pa.; and clerk in the Pension Office at Washington, D. C., from 1882 to 1885. Mr. Landis is yet a resident of the Capital city, although he has a farm at Landisville, this county.

Solon Z. Landis,[7] who lives on a farm at Maytown, this county, was married in 1878. He has one daughter named Pearle, born in August, 1879.

DESCENDANTS OF BENJAMIN.[5]

"Big" Benjamin Landis,[5] son of Hansle,[4] married Barbara Neff. They had nine children: John, Elizabeth, Esther, Susan, Henry, Catharine, Maria, Anna, and David. Benjamin resided in East Lampeter township, on the Horse-shoe road, and his occupation was farming. He died November 3, 1865. Barbara, his wife, died September 2, 1864.

John Landis,[6] of East Lampeter township, died in infancy.

Elizabeth Landis was married to Tobias Kreider, November 6, 1832; died, January 7, 1848.

Esther Landis was married to Abraham Landis, January 18, 1838.

Susan Landis was married to John Rohrer, November 5, 1840.

Henry Landis[6] was born January 25, 1808; married to Mary Johns, October 14, 1830. His wife was born on December 14, 1811; died, September 30, 1883. Henry resided in East Lampeter township; occupation, retired farmer.

Catharine Landis was married to Tobias Shenk, December 23, 1851; died, September 2, 1885.

Maria Landis died August 8, 1864; unmarried.

Anna Landis died October 31, 1870; unmarried.

David N. Landis[6] was born September 12, 1824; married to Catharine Martin, September 18, 1845. At one time he was associated with L. L. Kreider in general merchandise, at Witmer. Is now a farmer at Smoketown, East Lampeter township. His six children are: Catharine, Michael M., Eliza A., Elmina, Benjamin F. M., and Anna M.

Catharine Landis, oldest daughter of David N., was born February 26, 1826. Married to a Mr. Martin.

Michael M. Landis,[7] of East Lampeter township, was born November 3, 1846.

Eliza A. Landis was born June 17, 1850; married to John E. Ellsworth, October 13, 1875. Residence, Leacock township, near New Holland.

Elmina Landis was born September 19, 1852; married to Elam W. Leaman, December 4, 1871. Residence, near Gordonville, Leacock township.

Benjamin F. M. Landis[7] was born August 21, 1854. He has been studying art since 1873 in Europe. His residence is Munich, Bavaria, where he is engaged in his calling.

Anna M. Landis was born November 12, 1857; married to William D. Winger, September 2, 1882. Residence, Honeybrook, Chester county, Pa.

Peter Landis,[7] one of the sons of Henry,[6] was born March 11, 1833; married to Martha Barr, October 3, 1854. They had six children: Mary Ann (who died in infancy), Christian, Anna, Mary, Henry, and Eli B. Peter is a retired farmer living in East Lampeter township.

Christian Landis[8] was born October 10, 1856; married to Emma Rohrer, October 6, 1881. He is a graduate of Iron City Commercial College, Pittsburgh, Pa. Resides now at Mechanicsburg (Leacock post-office); occupation, farming.

Anna Landis was born July 27, 1858; married, November 22, 1877, to Joseph Leaman.

Mary Landis was born December 20, 1859; married to Benjamin Rohrer, December 16, 1880.

Henry Landis[8] was born October 20, 1861; married to Mary Groff, October 18, 1883. Residence, East Lampeter township; occupation, farmer.

Eli B. Landis[8] was born December 18, 1865. Educated in Millersville State Normal School and University of Pennsylvania, Philadelphia. Studied medicine with Dr. S. T. Davis, Lancaster; and is now completing his medical education in the Quaker city. He is unmarried.

DESCENDANTS OF HENRY.[5]

"Swamp" Henry Landis,[5] who was the youngest son of Hansle,[4] married Maria Rohrer, and resided on the "long lane," East Lampeter township. They had four children, two sons and two daughters: Christian R., David R., Mary R., and Lydia R. Mrs. Henry Landis died in East Lampeter, aged 66 years, 1 month and 19 days.

Christian R. Landis,[6] Leacock, was married to Hettie S. Landis. They had seven children, six sons and one daughter: Abraham L., Amos L., Henry L., Reuben L., Adam L., Milton L., and Lydia L. Christian has been a director of the Lancaster County National Bank; also, a School Director several times since 1854.

Henry L. Landis[7] was married to Mary Siegrist. They had two daughters: Hettie S. and Annie S.

Adam L. Landis was married to Lavinia Landis. They had one daughter, Ellenora L.

Milton L. Landis was married to Martha Becker. They had one son, Milton B.

Mary R. Landis, a daughter of "Swamp" Henry, was married to Christian S. Landis.

Lydia R. Landis was married to Jonas Buckwalter.

DESCENDANTS OF "BENNIE."[4]

"Bennie" Landis,[4] second son of Benjamin,[3] was married to Elizabeth Brackbill,* by whom he had three sons: John (Manor), Benjamin and Jacob (Ohio).

"Big" John Landis,[5] of Manor, was born in that township, on June 9, 1786. He spent his early years on his father's farm, where he assisted. Although the opportunities for ob-

---

* Elizabeth was the great-grandchild of Ulrich, the progenitor of the Brackbill family, who emigrated from Germany to this country, on August 24, 1717.

taining an education were limited at that time, he availed himself of such as were offered. At the age of nineteen he removed to Conestoga township to the farm now owned by his son Tobias, and the same year was married to Elizabeth Rudy, to whom were born: Benjamin, John, Veronica (Fannie), and Mary. By a second union with Anna Hoover (born April 2, 1787), his children were: Susan, Elizabeth, Jacob H., David (retired), Tobias H., and Magdalena. Mr. Landis was a man of enterprise and public spirit. He carried on both farming and milling about three miles west of Millersville. Was elected Supervisor of Conestoga township about 1817. When a resident of Manor, he served twice as County Commissioner—in 1838 and again in 1846. In politics he was a Whig, and subsequently a Republican, but not active in the political field. In his religious belief he was a consistent Mennonite until his death, which occurred August 22, 1870, in his eighty-fifth year. His first wife died in 1816; his second wife died in 1857.

Jacob H. Landis[6] came into existence in Conestoga township, April 18, 1822. On attaining his fourth year his parents removed to Manor township. During his youth he was a pupil at Lititz, and, also, at a select school in Manheim township. After becoming familiar with farm work he became an apprentice at milling in 1841; he soon afterward assumed the management of his father's mill. In 1861 he became sole proprietor of the mill and farm, which he conducted successfully until his retirement from business in 1880, when his sons relieved him. Mr. Landis was married to Anna S. Herr (born January 10, 1825), on February 26, 1852. Their children are: John H., Mary (Mrs. Wenger), Susan (Mrs. Reist), Lizzie (Mrs. Stebman), Fannie, and David H. Jacob H. is a Republican in politics, although no active partisan. He is, also, interested in education, and has been a trustee of the State Normal School, near his home, besides a School Director of his township. He and his wife are Mennonite in religion, though favorable to other denominations.

Hon. John H. Landis,[7] a son of Jacob H., was born in Manor township, January 31, 1853. Was educated in the common schools and at the Millersville State Normal School. Left school at the age of seventeen and learned milling, in

which business he has been engaged ever since, being proprietor of the Colfax Glen Mills at the present time. In 1876
he was elected President of the Lancaster County Lyceum
Association. In 1878 he was elected to the State Legislature
by the Republicans; was re-elected in 1880 and again in 1882,
serving as Chairman of the House Committee on Education
during the session of 1881. During the summer and fall of
1879 he traveled extensively through the western Territories
and the Pacific coast. Since the close of his legislative
career he has been prominently mentioned in connection with
the State Senatorship from the Southern district. He is President of the Agricultural and Horticultural Society of Lancaster County, President of the Manor Township Mutual Fire
Insurance Company, President of the Republican Anti-Cor-
ruption Association of Lancaster County (in which he is an
indomitable worker), a Director in the Northern National
Bank, of Lancaster, and a Manager in the Lancaster Chemical
Company (limited). On November 6, 1879, he was married to Bessie A. Thomas, of Ashland, Pa. Mrs. Landis
was born April 9, 1852, at Pottsville, Schuylkill county,
this State. They have two children: Anna Mary and Francis Thomas. The entire family belong to Zion's Reformed
church.

David Landis[6] married Fannie Mayer, of Manheim township. Their children are: Fannie, who lives with her
father, unmarried; and Amos M., who is married to Lizzie,
daughter of Rev. Amos Herr, West Lampeter township.
David is a retired farmer, and lives in a fine residence in the
village of Millersville.

Tobias H. Landis[6] is a bachelor and retired farmer, residing
at Millersville, this county.

Benjamin Landis,[5] second son of "Bennie,"[4] lived on the old
Manheim township homestead, and died in 1822. He leaves
grandsons near Neffsville.

Jacob Landis,[5] youngest son, moved to Ohio prior to 1870,
and was supposed to live there some years since. He has a
son in Kansas City, Mo., John K., who is said to have become
a man of note and wealth. The latter conducts an extensive
livery there.

DESCENDANTS OF "BLIND" HENRY.[4]

Henry Landis,[5] a son of "Blind" Henry (born December 5, 1760), was born and raised in Manheim township. He married Anna Long, also of that township. They lived on the Reading road (now Oregon turnpike). Had ten children who grew to maturity, and all were married except Mary, the youngest, who died single; they were named: Benjamin, John, Henry, Isaac, Jacob, Susan, Elizabeth, Nancy, Barbara, and Mary. Henry[5] was a farmer, and carried on distilling; had a team on the road constantly hauling his own whiskey and flour to Philadelphia. His oldest son Benjamin drove his team for four years; next John drove it three years; then Henry was his father's teamster, when Isaac and Jacob came in next for their turn of team-work up to the time they were married.

"Rich" Benjamin Landis,[6] the oldest son, was married to Nancy Long, of Manheim township, and lived near Oregon. They had eleven children, as follows: Henry, Isaac, Benjamin, Israel L., Daniel, Eliza, Fianna, Maria, Fanny, Nancy, and Amelia. They were all married and have children, except Israel, who is a bachelor.

Henry Landis[7] was married to Catharine Reist, of Warwick township. They have twelve children, all grown: Andrew R., Peter R., Henry R., Benjamin R., Isaac R., Jacob R. (married October 27, 1887, to Annie B. Hess, of Manheim township), Israel R., Annie, Lizzie, Katie, Ella, and Clara.

Isaac Landis[7] was married to Eliza Long, daughter of Benjamin Long, of Manheim township. They had one son when the mother died. Isaac married his second wife, Susan Landis, daughter of David and grand-daughter of "Farmer" John Landis. They have several children.

Daniel Landis[7] was married to a Miss Erb, of Warwick township. They had two children when Daniel died.

Eliza Landis married John Hess, at present residing at Roseville, Manheim township.

Fianna Landis married Benjamin Garber, near Donegal Springs.

Maria Landis married Levi Getz, a farmer, residing in East Hempfield township.

Fanny Landis married Samuel Hess, from Warwick township.

Nancy Landis married Samuel Hershey, now residing near Strasburg.

Amelia Landis married Michael Nolt, now residing on the old Hans Groff farm, in Groff"s Dale.

Benjamin Landis[7] married Mary Landis, daughter of David (she being a sister of Susan, his brother Isaac's wife). They have ten children living: Amelia, Maria (married to Ephraim Rohrer, farmer), Elim (married. to Miss Sheaffer, of Lampeter township), Lizzie (married to Harry Charles, farmer), Hetty (married to John Nolt, farmer), Alice, Annie, Laura, Martin, and Minnie.

Israel L. Landis[7] resides in Lancaster. He is an inventor, and actively engaged in the business of patent rights, including various useful farm gates. He gives part of his time to buying tobacco and looking after his farm. He is also largely interested in the affairs of one of the prominent banks of the city. Was born in Manheim township, February 25, 1836.

"Miller" John Landis,[6] son of Henry,[5] married Elizabeth, daughter of Michael Lane, Manheim township. They had six children, as follows: Abraham (miller, who died April 25, 1887, aged fifty-five, single), John (who died an infant), Henry (who was killed by lightning), Elizabeth (died in infancy), Michael (a bachelor, living on the old homestead near Oreville, East Hempfield township), and John, the youngest. The latter lives in Manheim township, and is married to Lydia Buckwalter, of that township. John[7] is engaged at farming. He and his brother Michael own a large grist mill at Oreville, on the Little Conestoga, which they are running in connection with their farms.

"Drover" Henry Landis[6] was married to Anna Stauffer, of Manheim township. They had three children when his wife died, who were named as follows: Emanuel (who died when 1 year and 8 months old), Fanny (married to David Graybill, now residing in East Petersburg; had two children, Susan and Henry, who both died young), and Anna, who married Levi S. Reist, of Warwick township; she had four children: Henry, who died quite young; Clara, wife of Henry Hostetter, of Manheim township; Laura, wife of Jacob F. Hess, of

Manheim township; Anna, the youngest daughter, died aged about 15. After remaining a widower three years, "Drover" Henry married his second wife, Esther Binkley, daughter of Christian Binkley.* Henry had two children with the latter union, who were named Elizabeth and Henry.

Elizabeth Landis[7] was married to Hon. John M. Stehman, Manheim township, at present residing in Rohrerstown. Elizabeth had one child, Henry L., and she died when her son was a little more than one year old. His grandmother took him in charge and kindly cared for him until he was able to care for himself. Henry L. Stehman married Lizzie Landis, daughter of Jacob Landis, residing at Millersville.

Henry H. Landis,[7] the youngest of the family, married Emma C. Diller, daughter of George Diller, of East Earl township. They have four children: Anna Margaretta, who died aged 4 years; Henry Kimper, now a student at Lehigh University; George Diller, at home with his father on the farm; Nettie May, the youngest, also at home.

Isaac Landis[6] married Mary Shirk, of Manheim township. They had four sons and two daughters. Isaac carried on the business of farming up to the time of his death, and was noted for feeding fine cattle. John S., the oldest son, was married to Anna Becker, daughter of Rev. Becker, a Mennonite minister, of Warwick township. Henry S. married Sarah Ford, of Manheim township. Joseph died single. Isaac[7] married Harriet Fry, from Ephrata; lives at Landis Valley and is engaged in farming. Maria is married to John Brubaker, of Manor township, son of Rev. Jacob Brubaker, a Mennonite minister. Fanny died single.

Jacob Landis,[6] the youngest son, married Elizabeth Binkley, of Manheim township, daughter of David Binkley. Jacob had three sons: David,[7] the oldest, was killed on the Pennsylvania Railroad. Benjamin[7] married Mary Buckwalter, of Manheim; they have five children, viz.: Phares, Amanda, Mabel, Mary, and Annie. Benjamin owns a farm and lives on it at Landis Valley. Henry, the youngest son, died single.

---

*Christian Binkley built the first arched stone bridge across the Conestoga, at the Printers' Paper Mill.

Nancy Landis[6] was married to Abraham Hershey, who carried on the milling business near Manheim; afterwards moved north of that borough, where he died, leaving eight children to grow up, all of whom are married: Eusebius Hershey, a Reformed Mennonite minister, now living in Centre county, this State. Fannie married Henry Zook, now residing in Lancaster city. Martha is married to Emanuel Longenecker, at present residing in Kansas. Nancy (Mumah) resides in Harrisburg; Mrs. Bowman lives in Lebanon county; Mary (Capp) is in Illinois; Barbara (Hernly) lives near Manheim; and Susanna (Minnich) is near Lititz. The husbands of the latter three daughters are farmers.

Elizabeth Landis[6] was married to a Mr. Bear, near Rohrerstown. She had two children, Christian and Barbara. Christian died single; Barbara married John L. Miller, now residing in Lancaster, engaged in the dry goods business. Elizabeth married a second time to Michael Martin, who was a farmer living near Roseville, Manheim township.

Barbara Landis[6] was married to Christian Brackbill, of Strasburg township, who owned a farm along the old Philadelphia pike, and, also, did a transportation business, controlling a warehouse and several cars on the Pennsylvania Railroad up to the time of his death. Barbara had four children: Henry L. Brackbill, now residing at Landis Valley, formerly of the Landis Valley hotel. (See Part IV.) Eliza Ann married John Risser, now living at Brunnerville, son of Rev. John Risser, a Mennonite minister. Christian is married to an Erb, and resides at Brunnerville. Maria died single.

DESCENDANTS OF BENJAMIN,[4] FARMER.

Benjamin Landis,[4] oldest son of Abraham,[3] lived on a farm in East Lampeter township. He had eight children, four sons and four daughters: John, Abraham, Benjamin, David, and Anna, Barbara, Susanna, and Mary—all now deceased. Benjamin[4] died about 1830.

"Farmer" John Landis,[5] oldest son of Benjamin,[4] was born in East Lampeter township, January 6, 1785. He was married to Eve Groff (born September 22, 1783). John was elected Commissioner for Lancaster county in 1846. He was, also, one of the originators of the Lancaster County Bank, of which he was the first President, after it became a chartered institution; elected to that office in 1841, and continued to fill the same honorably until February, 1867, a period of twenty-six years. John was a farmer by occupation. He had nine children: David G., Catharine G., Mary G., Susanna G., Elizabeth G., Esther G., Martin G., John G., and Anna G. "Farmer" John died February 4, 1867; his wife died November 25, 1877.

David G. Landis[6] was born January 19, 1809, in East Lampeter township. Married to Mary Neff, by whom he had four sons and six daughters: John, Christian, Soses, David, Susanna, Mary, Leau, Eveanna, Anna, and Lizzie. David G. was a farmer, and died on March 9, 1883.

John Landis,[7] son of David G., was married to Lizzie Rohrer. They have five sons and one daughter, all under age except Jason and Ellie.

Christian Landis[7] was married to Anna Leaman. They have one son and three daughters, all under age.

Soses (?) Landis has one daughter and two sons. The sons are farmers. All reside in East Lampeter.

David Landis had two daughters to first wife (Rohrer), and two sons to second (Catharine Landis). He resides in Upper Leacock, and is a farmer and butcher.

Susanna Landis was married to Isaac L. Landis, farmer, Manheim township.

Mary Landis married Benjamin L. Landis, farmer, Manheim township.

Leau Landis was married to Jacob Buckwalter, farmer, East Lampeter township.

Eveanna Landis married Adam Ranck, of Paradise township.

Anna Landis married Michael Rohrer, farmer, of Upper Leacock.

Lizzie Landis married Jacob Hostetter, farmer, of Manheim township.

Catharine G. Landis[6] was born on February 2, 1811. Married Jacob Rohrer. Died in Strasburg township, May 26, 1836.

Mary G. Landis was married to John Leaman. Died on May 13, 1846, in Leacock township.

Susanna G. Landis was born April 7, 1814. Married to Tobias Herr. Died, July 1, 1847, in Lancaster township.

Elizabeth G. Landis was born December 9, 1817. Married to John Doner, Manor township.

Esther G. Landis was born September 2, 1818. Married to Michael Metzger. Died, October 30, 1847, in Lampeter township.

Martin G. Landis[6] was born May 13, 1820. He is unmarried and resides in East Lampeter township.

John G. Landis[6] was born June 10, 1822. Married to Martha Barr. Died in Virginia about 1875. Left one daughter and two sons; one of the latter, John, resides in East Lampeter township.

Anna G. Landis[6] was born July 11, 1826. She is single and resides in East Lampeter township.

Abraham Landis,[5] second son of Benjamin,[4] lived and died in East Lampeter township.

Benjamin Landis,[5] third son, lived and died in the same township.

"Miller" David Landis[5] resided, also, in East Lampeter. He was a member of the board of Poor Directors in 1872.

DESCENDANTS OF "MUSSER" JOHN.[4]

"Musser" John Landis,[4] second son of Abraham,[3] resided in East Lampeter township. By his first wife (Musser) he had nine children, all of whom died in about one week from a fever. By a second marriage (Hoover) he had three sons and two daughters: John, Abraham, Emanuel, Annie, and Polly (Mrs. Rohrer).

John Landis,[5] oldest son, lived in East Lampeter township, and died about thirty years ago. Two of his sons, Adam and John S., are in the dairy business, near Lancaster city.

Abraham Landis[5] owned the farm near the water works, known as the "city mill farm," in Lancaster township. His children were: Eli, Mary, Susan, Harriet (Zook), and Philip.

Philip Landis[6] lived at the City Mill, Lancaster. He was married to Kate Gunkel. They removed to Delaware, living there seven years; and afterward came back to the farm at the old city water works, where they also resided seven years. Their children are: Jennie, Annie, William (Graymont, Ill.), and Victor. Philip is deceased, and his widow lives at No. 524 East Orange street, Lancaster.

Emanuel Landis[5] resides near the Pennsylvania Railroad bridge, on the Lampeter side of the Conestoga. His children include three boys and three girls: Samuel K., Levi K., Barbara (who was killed by being caught in machinery at Shober's mill, aged 22), Sarah, Henry, and Lydia.

Levi K. Landis[6] was born in East Lampeter township, on August 14, 1838. He learned the machinist trade; and about twenty-nine years since went to Lancaster, where he is yet located, on East King street. He had ten children, eight of whom are living: Addie, Levi (machinist), Ida, Charles C., George, Emery, Howard, and Blanche.

DESCENDANTS OF "BRICK" JOHN.[4]

"Brick" John Landis,[4] of Lampeter township, oldest son of Jacob,[3] was twice married. By his first wife (Burkholder) he had three children, two sons and one daughter, viz.: Jacob B., John B. and Nancy B.

Jacob B. Landis,[5] born October 21, 1792, was married to Maria Stauffer (born, August 15, 1797; died, July 18, 1865). They had six children, three sons and three daughters, viz.: Levi S., Anna S., Frances S., Maria S., Jacob S., and Christian S. Jacob B. died in East Lampeter township, near Landis' warehouse, on the P. R. R., January 24, 1835.

Levi S. Landis,[6] born January 31, 1830, oldest son of Jacob B., was married to Maria Andrews. They had four children: Elias (died in infancy), J. Franklin, Ezra A., and Ellenora (died aged about 12). The old homestead of Jacob,[3] third son of Benjamin,[2] passed down to Levi S.*

J. Franklin A. Landis[7] was married to Mary L. Leaman. They had three children, two sons and one daughter, viz.: A. Levi L., David L. and Stella L.

Ezra A. Landis[7] was married to Annie S. Lefevre. They had four children, two sons and two daughters, viz.: Elmer L., Harvey L., Arvilla L., and Bertha L.

---

*From whom it was purchased under influence of the P. R. R., at the time when the track was straightened east of the Conestoga bridge. The old homestead of Benjamin Landis[2] adjoins this on the east and is occupied by the Henry N. Landis family.

Anna S. Landis[6] was born October 23, 1821; died, May 6, 1848.

Frances S. Landis[6] was born August 28, 1824. She became the wife of Amos Bushong (born December 25, 1823), miller, at Bird-in-Hand. They had three children: Ira Clement (born, December 12, 1854; died, January 31, 1863), M. Viola* (born March 25, 1858), and Frank W.† (born March 17, 1864).

Maria S. Landis[6] was born October 17, 1826. She became the wife of Isaac D. Heller, and died in June, 1870.

Jacob S. Landis[6] was born March 27, 1829, and married to Lizzie Buckwalter. They had one daughter, Ada B., who married I. Newton Bushong, Bird-in-Hand. Mrs. Lizzie lives with her daughter. Jacob S. died February 4, 1863.

Christian S. Landis,[6] born March 29, 1833, was married to Sarah Cooper (whose second husband is Dr. Miller). They had one daughter, Mamie C., Bird-in-Hand. Christian S. died September 5, 1865.

John B. Landis,[5] second son of "Brick" John, was married to Martha Mylin. They had seven children, four sons and three daughters: Amos M., Daniel M., John M., Jacob M., Mary M., Susan M., and Eliza M. John B. lived and died in West Lampeter township, on the Millport and Strasburg turnpike.

Amos M. Landis,[6] first son of John B., was married to Hettie Rohrer. They had two children, one son and a daughter: John R. and Emma R.

Daniel M. Landis[6] was married to Christiana McCallister. They had two children, one son and a daughter: William and Henrietta.

Mary M. Landis was married to John Diffenbach.

Nancy B. Landis,[5] daughter of "Brick" John, was married to Abraham Shenk.

---

* Viola became the wife of D. B. Shuey, a graduate of Franklin & Marshall College and the Theological Seminary, Lancaster, and is now Superintendant of Missions of the Reformed church in the west. His home is Emporia, Kansas.

† F. W. Bushong graduated at F. & M. College, 1885. Spent two years at the University of Leipzig, Germany, and is at present Professor of Chemistry, Natural Science and the German Language in Wichita University, Wichita, Kansas.

"Brick" John Landis,[4] by his second marriage to Barbara Snavely (born, October 5, 1779; died, December 25, 1854), had eleven children, six sons and five daughters, viz.: Abraham S., Elizabeth S., Benjamin S., Christian S., Martin S., David S., Daniel S., Susan S., Barbara S., Mary S., and Hettie S.

"Old Road" Abraham S. Landis,[5] born July 2, 1798, was married to Barbara Landis (born, January 31, 1779; died, August 7, 1881), sister of "Farmer" John. They had nine children, two sons and seven daughters: John L., Barbara L., Mary L., Annie L., Elizabeth L., Hettie L., Susan L., Benjamin L., and Lydia L. Abraham died in East Lampeter township, November 12, 1874.

John L. Landis[6] (now deceased) was married to Elizabeth Musser. They had six children, three sons and three daughters: Abraham M., John M., Henry M., Barbara M., Mary M., and Susan M.

Abraham M. Landis[7] was married to Hettie W. Siegrist.

John M. Landis[7] was married to Emma M. Myers. They had one son, Abraham M.

Benjamin L. Landis,[6] son of Abraham S.,[5] was married to Fanny Bassler. They had seven children, two sons and five daughters, viz.: Abraham B., Benjamin B., Annie B., Fanny B., Lizzie B., Hettie B., and Barbara B.

Abraham B. Landis[7] was married to Ida B. Landis. They had one son, John-Jacob L.

Barbara L. Landis[6] was married to Joseph Leaman.

Annie L. Landis was married to John Kreider.

Elizabeth L. Landis was married to David Leaman.

Hettie L. Landis was married to Benjamin Groff.

Lydia L. Landis was married to John Groff.

Elizabeth S. Landis,[5] daughter of "Brick" John, died May 6, 1820, aged 20 years.

Benjamin S. Landis,[5] son of "Brick" John, was married to Mary Buckwalter, and resided in Upper Leacock, near Bareville. Had nine children, four sons and five daughters: Mary B., Elizabeth B., John B., Hettie B., David B., Fianna B., Benjamin B., Jacob B., and Harriet B.

Mary B. Landis[6] was married to Wayne Bear.

Elizabeth B. Landis was married to Samuel Weaver.

John B. Landis[6] was married to Maria Sheibley.

Hettie B. Landis was married to John Bear.

David Buckwalter Landis[6] was born in East Lampeter township, on January 13, 1830. Married to Martha Groff. Had one son, Clayton G. David sold his farm about a dozen years since, and now resides at No. 202 East King street, Lancaster. He has been a Director of the Inquirer Printing & Publishing Company for some years. Under the firm name of D. B. Landis & Son, he is actively engaged in merchant milling, at a large establishment located near the Pennsylvania Railroad and Quarryville branch of the Reading Railroad.

Fianna B. Landis was married to Abraham Grabill.

Harriet B. Landis was married to Isaac Sprecher.

Benjamin B. Landis was married to Barbara Groff. They had eight children, three sons and five daughters, viz.: Abraham G., Benjamin G., John G., Cassie G., Ida G., Cora G., Annie G., and Alice G.

Jacob B. Landis[6] was married to Mary Bender. They had five children, three daughters and two sons, viz.: Annetta B., Emma B., Ida B., Sanford B., and Theodore B.

Christian S. Landis,[5] son of "Brick" John, was married to Mary R. Landis, daughter of "Swamp" Henry. They had six children, two sons and four daughters, viz.: Levi L., Elizabeth L., Annie L., Katie L., John L., and Hettie L. Christian died in East Lampeter township, in 1871.

Levi L. Landis[6] was married to Mary Buckwalter. They had six children, one son and five daughters: Elam B., Hettie B., Amanda B., Emma B., Anna-Mary B., and Lydia B.

Elam B. Landis[7] was married to Martha Martin. They had six children, five daughters and one son: Mary M., Annie M., Emma M., Magdalena M., Ada Catharine M., and Harry M.

Elizabeth L. Landis[6] was married to Peter B. Brubaker.

Annie L. Landis was married to Peter E. Hershey.

Katie L. Landis was married to Christian S. Risser.

Rev. John L. Landis,[6] Binkley's Bridge, was married to Mary J. Denlinger. They had two children, one son and a daughter: Aaron D. and Annie D. John was ordained to the Old Mennonite ministry, at Mellinger's meeting-house, on

December 27, 1865; and now serves in the Strasburg bishop district, at Mellinger's and Stumptown.

Aaron D. Landis[7] was married to Annetta B. Landis. They had five children, one son and four daughters: Mary L., John L., Anna L., Ada L., and Emma L.

Susan S. Landis,[5] daughter of "Brick" John, was married to Michael Buckwalter.

Martin S. Landis,[5] son of "Brick" John, was born March 9, 1808. Married to Elizabeth Rupp (born January 13, 1814). They lived near Bareville. Had four children, two sons and two daughters: Abraham R., Samuel R., Amanda R., and Mary R.

Samuel R. Landis[6] was married to Annie Bassler.

Amanda R. Landis was married to Hershey Groff.

Mary R. Landis was married to Abraham S. Rohrer.

Barbara S. Landis,[5] daughter of "Brick" John, was married twice: 1. Jacob Stauffer; 2. John Leaman.

Mary S. Landis,[5] daughter of "Brick" John, was married to Emanuel Groff.

David S. Landis,[5] son of "Brick" John, was born April 2, 1814. Married to Elizabeth Hostetter; residence, Upper Leacock township. Had nine children, three sons and six daughters: John H., Jacob H., David H., Mary-Ann H., Hettie H., Ann Elizabeth H., Barbara H., Louisa H., and Catharine H.

Jacob H. Landis[6] was married to Lizzie B. Groff. They had seven children, six sons and one daughter: Elmer G., Milton G., David G., Ada G., Jacob G., Amos G., and Noah G.

Mary-Ann H. Landis was married to Jacob Metz.

Hettie H. Landis was married to Samuel Burkholder.

Ann Eliza H. Landis was married to John Wenger.

Barbara H. Landis was married to Abraham Kachel.

Louisa H. Landis was married to Abraham Herr.

Catharine H. Landis was married to David N. Landis.

Daniel S. Landis,[5] son of "Brick" John, was born April 2, 1814. Married to Elizabeth Hoover; residence, near East Petersburg. Had two sons: Jeremiah H. and Daniel H.

Jeremiah H. Landis[6] was married to Fanny Scheets. They had six children, three sons and three daughters: Lizzie S., Aaron S., Fanny S., Alvin S., Amanda S., and Jeremiah S.

Daniel H. Landis[6] was married to Leah Harnish. They had two children, one son and a daughter: Elmer H. and Sadie H.

Hettie S. Landis,[5] youngest daughter of "Brick" John, was married to Christian R. Landis.

DESCENDANTS OF ABRAHAM.[4]

Abraham Landis,[4] second son of Jacob,[3] was born November 1, 1767. He was twice married: 1. ——— Houser; 2. Elizabeth Breneman (born, August 11, 1775; married, 1795; died, November 15, 1857). Ten children were the result of these unions: Hettie, Nancy, Jacob, Maria, Elizabeth, Tobias, Abraham, Benjamin, Adam, and Rev. John B. Abraham[4] died March 10, 1851.

Hettie Landis[5] was born December 9, 1797; married to Abraham Siegrist.

Nancy Landis, was born November 4, 1801; married to Benjamin Stauffer.

"Gentleman" Jacob Landis,[5] the oldest son, was born November 2, 1803. Resided in East Lampeter township, and once was a Director of the Poor. He was married to Maria Hershey; and died March 10, 1879, leaving no children.

Maria Landis, born December 22, 1806; died, November 6, 1876.

Elizabeth Landis, born June 3, 1808; died, July 16, 1823.

Tobias Landis, born March 10, 1809; died, May 11, 1809.

Abraham Landis[5] (born, August 2, 1811; died, November 4, 1871) lived on the original Landis homestead. He was married to Hetty Landis (born November 28, 1814; now deceased), daughter of "Big" Benjamin, and their children are: Betsy, Mary, Benjamin, Jacob, and Abraham.

"Bush" Benjamin Landis[5] was born April 17, 1814. Resided, also, on the old Landis farm. He was married to Elizabeth Kreider. Their children are: Lizzie K., Mary K., Annie K., Fannie K., Hetty K., Abraham K., and Benjamin K. "Bush" Benjamin died July 8, 1884.

Elizabeth K. Landis,[6] oldest child of "Bush" Benjamin, became the wife of a Mr. Herr. They had four children: Annie (deceased), Elias, Lizzie, and Emma.

Mary K. Landis is married to a Kreider. They had four children: Infant son (deceased), Susan, Lizzie, and Mollie.

Annie K. Landis is now Mrs. Groff. Her children are: Lizzie, Emma, David, Annie, Benjamin, Ida, and Mollie.

Abraham K. Landis,[6] farmer, was married to Barbara Bear. They had eight children: Lizzie (deceased), three infants (deceased), Enos (deceased), Abraham, Ida, and Annie.

Fannie K. Landis was married to a Mr. Shaub. Their children include: Lizzie, Annie, Enos, Benjamin, Ellenora, Ada, and Mollie.

Hetty K. Landis became Mrs. Denlinger. She has one child, Benjamin.

Benjamin K. Landis,[6] youngest son of "Bush" Benjamin, was born July 1, 1855. He received a common school education. Was married to Maria V. Brackbill, on December 9, 1880. Is engaged at farming, near Bird-in-Hand, East Lampeter township. His children are: Infant son (deceased), born December 27, 1881; Elmer Park, born November 24, 1882; and Lillian Maud, born December 26, 1885. Mr. Landis has been a junior member, for several years, of the firm of Brackbill, Kendig & Landis,* Strasburg, who are extensive importers and breeders of thoroughbred Holland cattle. Is at present a School Director of his township.

Adam Landis[5] was born February 15, 1817, and lived in East Lampeter township. He married Sarah Overly (whose second husband was named Wikert). They had one son, Enos.

Rev. John B. Landis,[5] the youngest son of Abraham, was born March 5, 1820, and resides on a farm at East Petersburg, East Hempfield township. He was married to Anna Kreider, in 1844. On October 18, 1849, he was ordained to the Old Mennonite ministry, and has served his Master faithfully ever since in the Brubaker district. His children were: Elizabeth, Maria, Anna, Katie, Hetty, Fannie, and Jacob. John B.'s wife died in 1880, at the age of 60 years, 8 months and 25 days.

Elizabeth Landis,[6] first daughter of John B., married Israel F. Root, of Landisville; she died in August, 1886; no issue.

---

*This firm has been very successful, as is evidenced by the many premiums taken at county fairs for their excellent stock.

Maria Landis, second daughter, was married to Martin P. Swarr, of East Hempfield township. Their children are: Salome (Mrs. Aungst), Milton L., Harry, and Martin.

Anna Landis, third daughter, was married to Christian F. Charles. Their children are: Amos, Christian, Landis, and John.

Katie Landis, fourth daughter, was married to Benjamin Charles. Their children are: Ellen, Anna, John, Joseph, Benjamin, Fannie (deceased), Jacob, and Lizzie.

Hetty Landis, fifth daughter, married to John M. Denlinger. Their children are: Landis, Benjamin and Harry.

Fannie Landis, sixth daughter, was married to Daniel H. Denlinger. Their children are: Lizzie, Daniel and Fannie.

Jacob Landis,[6] only son of John B., was married to Mary E. Kreider; no children.

Hettie Landis,[5] sixth child of Abraham, was married to Christian Siegrist. Their children are: John, Abraham, Christian, Jacob, Fannie, Hetty, Mary, Lizzie, and Anna.

Nancy Landis, seventh child, was married to Benjamin Stauffer. Their children are: Betsy, Fannie, Maria, John, Abraham, Peter, Benjamin, Adam, and Levi.

Mary Landis,[5] youngest daughter, was married to Tobias Kreider. Their children are: Jacob, Abraham and Mary.

DESCENDANTS OF HENRY.[3]

Benjamin Landis,[4] oldest son of Henry,[3] had four sons: Daniel, Henry, Benjamin, and John. All of these were born and resided part of their time about New Holland.

Daniel and Henry Landis[5] died at their home years ago.

Benjamin Landis moved to Adams county, near Gettysburg, this State, many years ago.

John Landis,[5] the youngest son, also moved to Adams county, near Gettysburg.

John Landis,[4] second son of Henry,[3] had two sons: "Little" Benjamin and John.

"Little" Benjamin Landis[5] resided in East Lampeter township, and died there.

John Landis,[5] the younger son, died at the age of 18, many years ago.

Henry Landis,[4] third son of Henry, had four sons: Daniel, Jacob, Henry, and Isaac.

Daniel Landis[5] lived in Manheim township, on the New Holland turnpike.

Henry Landis died in East Lampeter township; unmarried.

Isaac Landis lived in East Lampeter township, near Landis' store.

Jacob Landis died unmarried, in the same neighborhood.

Peter Landis,[4] fourth son of Henry, had one son: "Fuller" David, who resided in Upper Leacock township, near Monterey.

Rev. Abraham Landis,[4] youngest son of Henry,[3] lived and died upon what is part of the original Landis homestead, in East Lampeter township. He was a Reformed Mennonite minister and much esteemed for his worth as a citizen and a Christian. He had five sons and two daughters: Henry N., Abraham N., Jacob N., John N., Benjamin N., Mary N., and Anna N. Rev. Abraham died in 1861, aged 81 years.

Henry N. Landis,[5] the oldest, owns the old homestead in East Lampeter township. His children are: Abram S., Jacob S., Henry, of Reading, Pa. (see practitioners in medicine, Part VI.); Esther, and Annie (wife of John Light).

Abram S. Landis[6] has one child, Allen.

Jacob S. Landis'[6] children are: Frank, Anna, John, Henry, Omer, Emma, Alice, and Willis.

Esther Landis[6] married Andrew M. Frantz, esq., of Lancaster. Their children are: Lettie, Christian (deceased), Harry, and Lillie.

Abraham N. Landis[5] emigrated to Illinois in 1849, and settled in Whiteside county, near Sterling. His children are: John, Chicago, Ill.; Benjamin, Minneapolis, Minn.; Mary (Getz), Sterling, Ill.; Hattie (Stillman), deceased; Abram and Henry (married to Miss Summy).

Jacob N. Landis moved to Illinois, and died there about 27 years ago.

John N. Landis also moved to Illinois, and died there about 30 years since. His children were: Anna (married to Isaac Kreider), Eliza (married to Rev. Henry Fisher), Naomi (deceased), Fannie, Noah, and Jacob.

Benjamin N. Landis,[5] the youngest, removed to Franklin county, this State, and died there many years ago. He was married to Lydia Frick, daughter of Jacob Frick, of Neffsville, Lancaster county. Their children are: Frank F., Ezra F., Mary F., Salome F., Lizzie, Abram B., and Emma F.

Frank F. Landis[6] married Lizzie Hershey, of Mount Joy. He is a designer of machines with the Geiser Manufacturing Company, Waynesboro, this State. Children: Ida, Benjamin (deceased), Mary (deceased), Anna, Frank (deceased), Mark, and Lizzie.

Ezra F. Landis,[6] at the age of 17, became an apprentice for three years in George Frick's shops, Waynesboro, this State. He afterward went to Lancaster and established a machine shop of his own. Was married to Kate Anthes, of Port Coleborne, Ontario. His children are: Charles A., born July 10, 1873; Amelia A., born January 3, 1875; Grace Elizabeth, born June 27, 1877; Edith A., born September 11, 1879; Mary, born July 9, 1881; Adrienne, born July 26, 1883; and Catharine May, born May 17, 1885. Mr. Landis has managed an extensive trade in fan blowers, steam pumps, machines, and radiators, upwards of twenty years, in which he has been very successful. Both he and his wife are members of the Reformed Mennonite church.

Mary F. Landis[6] was married to Jacob D. Kohr, Dillerville, son of Bishop John Kohr, deceased. Children: Frank, Anna, Alice, Howard, Esther, and Lydia.

Salome F. Landis[6] became the wife of Jacob Miller, Ringgold, Md. Children: Mary, Anna, Lydia, and Lizzie.

Lizzie Landis[6] was married to Eli J. Treichler, of Sanborne, Niagara county, N. Y. Children: Charles, Mary, Lorine, Wilber, Elma, and several others.

Abram Landis[6] is a mechanical engineer at the Geiser Manufacturing Company's works, Waynesboro, this State. Was married to Leah H. Landis. Children: Mary (deceased), Mark (deceased), Benjamin, Harry, and Ruth.

Mary N. Landis[5] was married to Isaac Hershey (now deceased), Campbellstown, Dauphin county, this State. Children: Israel and Anna.

Anna N. Landis,[5] widow of Jacob Frantz, Waynesboro, Franklin county, this State. No children.

LINEAL DESCENDANTS OF FELIX,[1] OF DAUPHIN.

Felix Landis[3] was married and lived in the vicinity of Harrisburg, this State. One of his sons, Solomon, was married to a Miss Swartz, and lived about five miles east of Harrisburg, from whence he removed to near Balsbach's hotel—afterward going to Middletown, where he is reported as committing suicide by shooting himself.

The Spring Creek Landis relationship, of Dauphin county, claim that Felix[3] was a cousin* to the first three members of that family, of which there is any obtainable information. The genealogy of the "Spring Creek" family is, therefore, given herewith:

THE SPRING CREEK FAMILY.

John Landis[3] was the father of six children: Peter, John, Isaac, Nancy, Elizabeth, and Catharine. John (the father) died at the age of 75 years; his body is buried in Dauphin county.

Peter Landis[4] was married to a Miss Wisor. He died at the age of 69 years.

John Landis[4] died at the age of 68 years.

Isaac Landis[4] was married. Had one son of which there is any knowledge, named Joseph.

Joseph Landis[5] was born in 1822. Married to Catharine Reitzel. Is a farmer by occupation, and a resident of Conoy township, Lancaster county. Ten children comprise the family: Josiah, Christian, Mary, Joseph, Benjamin, Henry, Fanny, John, Abraham, and Catharine.

Josiah Landis,[6] the oldest, was born in 1846. Married to Catharine Rutt.

Christian Landis[6] was born in 1847. Married.

Mary Landis was born in 1849. Deceased.

Joseph Landis was born in 1851. Deceased.

Benjamin Landis was born in 1853. Unmarried.

Henry Landis was born in 1856. Married and moved to the State of Ohio.

* Based upon information collected by John F. Landis, of near Elizabethtown, Lancaster county.

Fanny Landis was born in 1859. Married Eli Huber.

John Landis was born in 1860. Left his home for some time past, no information as to his whereabouts ever being received by his parents.

Abraham Landis was born in 1861. Deceased.

Catharine Landis was born in 1863. Deceased.

Nancy Landis,[4] daughter of John,[3] was married to a Mr. Long.

Elizabeth Landis[4] was married to a Mr. Wolf.

Catharine Landis[4] was married to Joseph Brestel. She died at the age of 84 years.

Henry Landis,[3] brother of John (third generation of Felix), was married and the father of three sons, viz.: Abraham, John and Henry.

Christian Landis,[3] brother of John, had a family of two sons: David and Christian.

David Landis[4] moved to Carlisle, this State, where he died.

Christian Landis[4] was married, and had five children: Benjamin, David, Christian, Susanna (Barsht), and Mary (married to Benjamin Shoe).

DESCENDANTS OF HENRY, OF DAUPHIN.

Henry Landis,[1] who no doubt was a resident* of Dauphin county, as his numerous relations are now mostly located there, it is claimed was one of a family from which the Spring Creek Landises sprung at an early day during the last century. He was married to a Miss Bureman, by whom he had seven children: Peter B., Christopher, Jacob B., Henry B., Elizabeth B., Anna B., and John B.

Peter B. Landis,[2] the first member of the second generation, was married to a Miss Lauman (supposed to be related to the Lauman family of Middletown, Dauphin county). Peter moved to New York State. Nothing further is known of his family except about one son, George L. Landis, who was a Justice of the Peace.

---

* Henry's grave cannot be found among those of his family buried at what is known as Strickler's graveyard, Dauphin county, Pa.

Christopher Landis[2] was born August 27, 1770. Died, unmarried, while living with brother his John, on July 13, 1830, aged 59 years, 10 months and 16 days.

Jacob B. Landis,[2] of Dauphin county, was born May 9, 1781. Died, unmarried, on February 3, 1806, aged 24 years, 9 months and 24 days.

Henry B. Landis[2] was born May 10, 17—. He was a resident of Dauphin county, near a cave along the banks of the Swatara creek, about one mile from Hummelstown. Had four sons, viz.: John, Jacob, Henry, and Joseph. Henry B. and his wife belonged to the Lutheran church. He was a firm believer in the Divine truth; and, after being nearly blind, through partial loss of sight, by constant prayer and undergoing two separate operations, he became more steadfast than ever. Died April, 1839, aged 49 years and some days.

John Landis[3] was born on October 15, 1805, one mile from Hummelstown, Dauphin county. According to the preface of a book of "Discourses on the Depravity of the Human Family,"* he was the "seventh child" of his parents. From childhood his disposition was more or less sedate and retiring. He was educated in a common country school; and early proved himself to be an adept in arithmetic, together with mensuration, surveying and gauging. His genius developed itself, also, in other ways; the gift of drawing and painting manifesting itself in youth. In fact, his life from childood was somewhat romantic. At about the age of 15, he attended the village church, with others; his mind became serious and more abstracted from earthly things, and he committed passages of Scripture with such delight and facility that one of his sisters wanted him to study for the ministry. He became a member of the Lutheran church. Afterward, however, he concluded to learn a trade, and accordingly apprenticed himself to Mr. Wyeth at Harrisburg until he was of age. In the winter of 1822–3 he began his career as a printer. He made rapid progress; in his own language he says: "The first day it was late when I got there, but I learned the cases and composed nearly half a

* Written by John Landis, and printed at Harrisburg, Pa., in 1839, by R. S. Elliott & Co.; 177 pp.

column of matter, long primer, for the paper." He continued
to study his Bible; but became a Sabbath-breaker, "and for
money would work all Sunday until night on the bills of the
Senate which Mr. Wyeth had engaged to print." Soon afterward he was taken with a fever and lay seriously ill for some
weeks. During this time his religious feelings again over-
took him, and while in a disturbed state of mind he resolved
to lead a better life. In a bit of verse he alludes to this thus:

> "And when this frame press'd with sickness,
> Sore disease and deep distress;
> The groan of anguish Thou didst hear,
> And lend'st Thyself a willing ear;
> To defeat the grave of its prey,
> Did'st Thy Almighty power display;
> To health again for to restore,
> That I might know Thee more and more."

After an absence of about ten weeks he returned to Mr.
Wyeth. A few weeks after leaving that printer's employ, he
became a partner in one of the first Jackson papers in the
State, printed at Reading, where he was six months. He
then sold his interest, and visited Philadelphia and New York,
working some weeks in the metropolis; also worked at Lancaster, York and divers other towns. Studied medicine six
months with an eminent physician; was successful, but the
practical part not being congenial to him, he left the profession and engaged in the brokerage business. Here again he
had considerable success, and accumulated a small fortune in
a few years. His sole object then was money, until he began
the study of painting, in the spring of 1830, under some
slight instruction of a local portrait painter. He then visited
Philadelphia, New York, Baltimore, and Washington, at different times, to examine the best pictures from the Italian
masters, besides those of West and other American artists.
In less than a year's time, after producing fourteen small single portraits, he began a vast design of "Christ Preaching
and Healing Diseases;"* this was commented upon by one of
the Philadelphia papers, where it was once on exhibition, as
indicating "an indubitable and high order of genius." Some

---

* This production was burned in the Lutheran church of Harrisburg,
in October, 1838, when that edifice was consumed.

other designs were named: "The Head of John the Baptist" (afterward exhibited in the Royal Exhibition, Pall Mall), "The Battle of New Orleans" (size of canvas 14 by 22 feet, with life-size figures), "St. Peter's Release by an Angel," etc. On August 1, 1833, he left for Europe; and, after a voyage of 42 days, he stepped on Brittania's shore at Liverpool. Took a stage for London, and located himself in the western part of the great city, where he pursued the study of his profession. During some unguarded moments, and for some unaccountable cause he was deprived of his personal liberty and imprisoned for at least two years. His religious knowledge there again manifested itself, and he wrote upwards of 200 hymns. In March, 1836, he left London and embarked for America, where he arrived in May. Here he pursued his studies as historical painter, and, also, wrote a poem entitled "Messiah," with a large number of verses. While in Chambersburg during the following year, he met with considerable success. He was the author of "A Soul's Aid," etc. There is, unfortunately, no record obtainable of his death or age.

Jacob Landis[3] was married and resided in Millersburg, this State.

Henry Landis was a resident of Franklin county, this State, where he died.

Joseph Landis moved to Indianapolis, Indiana.

Anna B. Landis[2] it is said was married. Died May 23, 1818, aged 72 years and 5 months. Buried in Strickler's graveyard, Dauphin county.

John B. Landis[2] was born in Dauphin county, August 17, 1775. He was married to Elizabeth Rutt (the first wife of Martin Nissley, Dauphin county). They had five children: John R., Elizabeth R., Anna R., Christian R., and Moses R. John B. died January 31, 1854, aged 78 years, 4 months and 14 days.

John Rutt Landis[3] was born January 28, 1808. He was married to Elizabeth Ebersole, February 10, 1843. His occupation was farming. Had six children, viz.: Henry E., Frances E., John, Jacob, David, and Lizzie. Died in Conoy township, Lancaster county, January 17, 1877, aged 68 years, 11 months and 27 days.

Henry Ebersole Landis[4] was born February 13, 1844. Married to Esther Longenecker, October 14, 1866. She was born November 27, 1845. They are the parents of six children, viz.: Anna Longenecker, born September 14, 1867; Jonas L., born November 2, 1869; Mary, born December 9, 1873; Lizzie, born October 20, 1875; Alice and Emma, twins, born August 28, 1881. Emma died June 13, 1882, aged 9 months and 15 days. Henry was a farmer near Bainbridge, Conoy township, Lancaster county.

Frances E. Landis,[4] twin sister of Henry E., was born February 13, 1844. Married to David M. Ebersole, September, 1869. They occupy a farm near Conewago, West Donegal township, Lancaster county. Their children are: Amanda L., born August, 1870; Levi L., born July, 1872; Anna L., born October 22, 1874.

John E. Landis[4] was born July 1, 1846. Married to Martha Bossler (born November 27, 1845), September 27, 1868. They are the parents of seven children, viz.: Ezra B., born March 29, 1871; Lizzie B., born April 30, 1873; Simon, born July 3, 1875; Ellen, born May 1, 1877; Mary Ann, born January 5, 1879; Martha, born August 5, 1880; and Malinda, born October 21, 1882. John carries on farming near Bainbridge, Conoy township, Lancaster county.

Jacob E. Landis[4] was born November 16, 1848. Married to Catharine, daughter of Rev. Benjamin Lehman, of Mount Joy township, Lancaster county. They have three children, viz.: John L., born July 4, 1878; Benjamin L., born November 15, 1879; and Jacob, born July 5, 1881. Jacob E. is a farmer near Bainbridge, Conoy township, Lancaster county.

David E. Landis[4] was born January 17, 1851. Married to Leah Bossler, sister of his brother John's wife, October 13, 1872. She died October 2, 1878, aged 33 years, 1 month and 7 days. They were the parents of four children: Amanda Bossler, born November 25, 1874; Elmer B., born April 27, 1876 (deceased); a daughter (deceased), born February 13, 1877; and David, born October 2, 1878. David E. was again married to Susanna R. (born May 9, 1850), daughter of Joseph Bucher, of Warwick township, Lancaster county, on October 26, 1882. By this union he had three children: Joseph Bucher, born March 1, 1884; Barbara B., born January 5, 1886; and Katie, born March 4, 1887. David's occupation is farming near Bainbridge, West Donegal township, this county.

Lizzie E. Landis[4] was born May 28, 1855. Married to Anderson Boll (born July 11, 1856), on September 5, 1878. Mr. B. works at railroad repairs and lives near Conewago, West Donegal township, Lancaster county. They have four children: John L., born June 2, 1879; Amos L., born February 5, 1881; Ervin L., born August 15, 1884; and Esther Elizabeth L., born June 14, 1886.

Elizabeth R. Landis[3] was born in Dauphin county. Married to Christian Risser. They were the parents of three daughters: Elizabeth L. (married to Jacob Lehman), Mary L. (wife of John Lehman) and Catharine L. (married to John Welker).

Anna R. Landis[3] was born March 5, 1812. She was married to John Wisler, and died March 12, 1853, aged 41 years and 10 days. They have five children: John L., Middletown; Mary L. (Ensminger); Solomon L., farming on an island in the Susquehanna River; Abraham (deceased), and Lizzie (deceased).

Christian R. Landis[3] was born in Derry township, Dauphin county, January 25, 1816. He went to Green township, Franklin county, this State, in 1842, where he was married December 7, 1845, to Susanna, daughter of Rev. John Lehman, a Mennonite minister. They are the parents of four children: John L., born December 9, 1846 (married); Daniel L., born March 31, 1852 (married); David L., born January 27, 1855 (married); and Christian L., born April 29, 1859 (married).

Moses R. Landis,[3] youngest son of John B,[2] was born September 19, 1819. Married to Elizabeth Keller, October 10, 1850. They resided in Dauphin county and are the parents of ten children: Mary Ann K., Samuel K., Jacob K., John K., Sarah Ann K., Joseph K., Henry K., Katie K., Martin K., and Elizabeth K.

Mary Ann K Landis[4] was born in 1851, and died August 1, 1853.

Samuel K. Landis[4] was born August 30, 1852. Married to Fannie E. Ebersole. They have one daughter, Fannie E.

Jacob K. Landis[4] was born August 13, 1854. Died in 1872, aged 17 years, 4 months and some days.

John K. Landis[4] was born February 21, 1856. Married to Sadie Gruber. They have four children: Minnie G., Annie G., Samuel G., and Sadie G.

Sarah Ann K. Landis[4] was born October 11, 1857. Married to William Beamesderfer. They have two sons: Martin L. and Harry L.

Joseph K. Landis[4] was born August 27, 1859. Married to Mary Fahs. They have three sons: Jacob F. (died at the age of 10 months), Harry F. and Joseph F.

Henry K. Landis[4] was born October 15, 1861. Married and has a family of two children: John and Emma.

Katie K. Landis was born March 12, 1863. Married to Samuel Lehman. They have one daughter, Amanda.

Martin K. Landis[4] was born December 6, 1865. Married to Carrie Shenk. They have one son, Franklin S.

Elizabeth K. Landis[4] was born May 29, 1866.

LINEAL DESCENDANTS OF JOHN,[1] OF BUCKS.

John Landis,[3] a grandson of John,[1] of Bucks county, was born August 16, 1776, and emigrated to Lancaster in 1797. He was married to a daughter of Michael Kline, grandfather of G. M. Kline, esq., of that city. In 1805 he removed to Middletown, and a year or two later he returned to Lancaster. He kept a store on East King street fourteen years; afterward on North Queen until 1829, when he removed to Warwick township. He returned again to the city about 1840, and was elected Alderman of the old North-east Ward, serving from February 26, 1842. He was made a Mason in Lodge No. 43, on May 13, 1818; was elected Senior Warden in 1824, and Worshipful Master in December, 1828, serving as such one year. He was also a member of Chapter No. 43, Royal Arch Masons. Died April 28, 1850.

Jesse Landis, esq.,[4] son of John,[3] was born October 15, 1821. Married Anna Jefferis, daughter of Joseph Jefferis, of Chester county, on December 4, 1847. She died January 3, 1848, one month after her marriage, aged 23 years. Mr. Landis was again married on October 15, 1850, to Elizabeth P. Daniel, daughter of 'Squire James Daniel, of Chester county. Six children were born of this union, all of whom are living: Mary E., Jessie E., Beulah G., Charles I., Matilda B., and James D. Jesse read law with Emanuel C. Reigart, esq., and was admitted to the bar on September 13, 1843. He was an attentive student and ranked among the well-read attorneys of the Lancaster bar. In 1861 he was elected by the Commissioners as County Solicitor, and held that office by successive re-elections until 1869. He was President of the American Fire Engine and Hose Company, Lancaster city, in 1862. He prepared a supplement to "Lynn's Analytical Index," a work of value to the profession, which was published in 1873. He died December 28, 1873. His wife, Elizabeth, still survives in vigorous health.

Mary E. Landis,[5] daughter of Jesse, is now the wife of Frank A. Diffenderfer, of Philadelphia.

Jessie E. Landis[5] is married to John R. Kauffman, druggist, Lancaster city.

Beulah G. Landis[5] is the wife of B. S. Schindle, business manager of the *New Era*, Lancaster.

Charles I. Landis, esq.,[5] was born in Lancaster, November 18, 1856. He was educated in the public schools of the city, and, also, for several years a student at Franklin & Marshall College. After teaching for several terms he took up the study of law with D. G. Eshleman, esq., being admitted to the bar in 1877. By close application he has forged his way to the front rank of the members of the bar. Mr. Landis is an ardent Republican, and as such was elected City Solicitor for one term. He was, also, for two years Chairman of the Republican County Committee. In addition to the duties of his profession, he is interested in various business enterprises, being Treasurer of the Lancaster Chemical Company, and Secretary of the Helvetia Leather Belting Company. He has, also, until recently, been one of the editors of the Lancaster *Law Review*.

James D. Landis[5] was born in Lancaster, March 14, 1862. He was educated in the common schools of the city, and engaged early in newspaper work. His first business connection was with the *Examiner and Express;* but at the organization of the *New Era* he engaged himself with that establishment, where he still remains, being managing editor of that journal. Mr. Landis is a Republican, and as such is an active worker for the interests of the Young Republicans, a prominent political organization of Lancaster city.

Joseph Landis[3] was born in 1784. He and his brother John moved to Lancaster county when they were young men. Joseph was married to Catharine Share, at what is now known as Redsecker's mill, Elizabethtown.

Josiah Landis,[4] a son of Joseph's, was born in 1822. He was married in 1853, and is now engaged in the drug business in Manheim, Lancaster county. No children living.

THE EPHRATA STOCK.

John Landis, of the second generation of the old Ephrata stock, was a pioneer farmer. He married a Miss Mohler, and had a patriarchal family of children. Among these were Abraham, who succeeded his father on the old homestead; David, of West Cocalico township; Elizabeth, who married John Shurr (and resided where Jacob W. Landis' tenant house now is); and Jacob.

David Landis[3] was "a soldier of the Revolution,"* who enlisted when very young and "served faithfully till the termination of the struggle, a period of five years and seven months." He was engaged in agricultural pursuits; and had possessions in West Cocalico township, at what is now Stevens, on Steinmetz's run. In 1780 he was assessed, as a freeholder, for 66 acres, 2 horses, 2 cows; value £254, tax £66. In 1824 he was elected from Ephrata township a member of the Legislature. He died April 7, 1852, aged ninety years.

Samuel Landis,[4] of Ephrata, a son of David,[3] was a member of the State Legislature in 1829 and '30. A son of his was popularly known as "Tragedian" Landis.

Jacob Landis[3] married Elizabeth Mellinger. Four of their children grew to maturity: Maria, Elizabeth, Anna, and Jacob, jr. None of these married except the latter son.

Jacob Landis[4] passed his life-time in a plain and industrious manner on the old homestead. He married Magdalena, daughter of Jacob Wissler, of Ephrata township, and had three children who attained adult years, viz.: Elizabeth, who

---

* Harris' Biographical History of Lancaster County.

became the wife of Levi Landis, of Ephrata township; Jacob W., and Mary, widow of Simon P. A. Weidman, a deceased merchant of Clay township. Jacob[4] died August 30, 1876.

Jacob Wissler Landis[5] was born on the farm where he now resides, in Ephrata township, on November 2, 1834. He enjoyed a common-school education and spent his earlier years as an assistant on his father's farm. After his father's death he came into possession of the farm. He is well known as a dealer in horses. As a public-spirited man he has been a member of the board of Directors of the Ephrata National Bank since the organization of that institution in 1881. He married Sarah Fry, and has six children: Alma, J. Harlan, Annie C. (married on September 13, 1887, to Martin H. Shirk, of Lincoln), Jacob C., Emma, and Charles S. Mr. Landis was elected in 1887 a delegate to the Republican State Convention from the Northern Representative District of this county.

Among the list of taxables comprising that portion of old Cocalico township now embraced in Ephrata township, are the following for 1780: Benjamin Landis, 78 acres, 2 horses and 2 cows, £260; Jacob Landis,* 118 acres, 2 horses and 3 cows, £265; John Landis,† 150 acres, 2 horses and 5 cows, £484; and John Landis, jr., East Cocalico township, 50 acres, 2 horses and 1 cow, £173.

Among those who subscribed to the oath of allegiance or fidelity, at Ephrata, during the Revolutionary War were: John, Abraham and Jacob Landis.

Some of the early members of the Seventh Day Baptists at Ephrata were named Landis. Ann Landis was a "sister" there during the Revolutionary War.

Abraham Landis, who owned Fahnestock's mill, was the founder of Landisburg, Perry county, this State (see Part VI).

Some of this stock still reside in Rothsville and Ephrata; others in York county, this State, and Montgomery county, Ohio.

---

*Jacob's second wife was, no doubt, named Salome. Among their children were: Catharine and Rebecca. John was a son of the first wife.
† His Will supposed to be filed in 1801.

DESCENDANTS OF ABRAHAM, NEAR EPHRATA.

Abraham Landis[1] was born near Ephrata, November 27, 1789. He was married to Mary Keller, and resided at Springville, then Ephrata township, Lancaster county. His occupation was that of a farmer, and, also, manufacturer of organs, spinning wheels, etc. Five sons were born to him, viz.: Samuel K., John K., Jacob K., Reuben K., and William K. Abraham died February 18, 1864.

Samuel K. Landis[2] was born in 1813. Married to Elizabeth Wolf, of near Ephrata; at present residing at Richland, Lebanon county. Three sons were born to them: Edwin W., queensware dealer, Reading; Abraham W., produce dealer, Richland (one son, a printer, being named Monroe R.); and Martin W. (who died in 1860).

John K. Landis[2] was born in 1815. Married to Harriet Royer (now deceased), of Mount Joy, this county. He resides at present at Ephrata. Three sons and two daughters were born to him: Edward, Franklin (deceased), Aaron, Fianna (deceased), and Mary.

Jacob K. Landis[2] was born in 1817. Married to Mary Shaeffer (deceased), Akron, this county. Resides at present at Richland, Lebanon county. Three sons and two daughters were born to him: Harrison, Franklin (operator, Richland), Jeremiah (deceased), Eliza, and Rebecca.

Reuben K. Landis[2] was born in 1819. Married to Sallie Shirk, Springville, this county. Now residing at Canton, Ohio. Children: Henry, Reuben (deceased) and Salinda.

William K. Landis was born in 1821. Married to Mary Deppen (deceased), Robesonia, Berks county, this State. Their children were: Levi D. (jeweler, Richland), Mary Ann, Emmaline, and Sarah (deceased).

LINEAL DESCENDANTS OF "HILL" JOHN.

About a score of years prior to the Revolutionary War, a man named John Landis[1] (whose descendants are known as the "Hill" family) occupied a farm lying on the south side of a hill,* about a-half mile south of a small village called

---

* On account of that hill the family was afterward so named.

"Fiddlers' Green" (since named Neffsville), Manheim township, Lancaster county. John married Mary Erb. They had four sons and one daughter: John E., Henry E. (married to Mary Wolf), David E. (married), Abraham E. (married to Mary Meyers), and Nancy E. Landis (married to a Lichty).

"Hill" John Landis,[2] son of John,[1] was born in Manheim township, on April 18, 1779. He became a resident of his father's farm for his life-time. Married to Margaretta Snavely, May 20, 1800. He was the father of four sons and seven daughters: Elizabeth S., John S., Mary, David, Margaret, Anna, Jacob, Henry, Leah, Magdalena, and Susanna. Mr. Landis died January 23, 1858; aged 78 years, 8 months and 5 days. His wife, who was born August 19, 1783, died August 24, 1855; aged 71 years, 11 months and 5 days.

Elizabeth Snavely Landis,[3] first daughter of John, was born December 7, 1801. Married to Jacob Stoner, farmer, who lived on the Lancaster & Lititz pike, Manheim township. She was the mother of seven sons and three daughters, viz.: Anna L. (Ephrata), Emanuel L., Jacob, Eliza L., John L. (East Petersburg), Isaac L. (Lincoln), David L. (Neffsville), Abraham L. (Roseville), Daniel L. (Coleraine township), and Maria L.

John S. Landis,[3] first son of John,[2] was born June 2, 1803. Married to a Miss Heise, August 18, 1825. They had one son, Jacob, when Mrs. L. died. He was again married to Anna Frankfort, of Lancaster city, August 18, 1830. By this last union their children were: Henry F., Elizabeth F., Mary F., Daniel F., Hettie F., Susanna F., John F., and Sarah Ann F. He died March 31, 1871, aged 68 years, 2 months and 28 days.

Jacob Heise Landis,[4] only son of the first wife of John S.,[3] was born June 22, 1827. He lived in the country until he was seventeen and a-half years old, after which he served an apprenticeship of three years and six months at carpentry, with Michael and Daniel Erisman. In 1850, in his twenty-third year, he was married to Elizabeth Kuhns, probably of Lancaster city; she died, without issue, November 26, 1860. Mr. Landis worked at his trade in Lancaster until February 11, 1862, when he left for Dayton, Ohio. Went to work there at his trade on the 13th of the same month, and kept at it until 1869, when he accepted a foremanship in D. E. McSherry's grain drill works, remaining there until June 1, 1887, after which he resigned at the age of 50 years. He was again married to Laura V. Staley, of Ohio.

Henry Frankfort Landis[4] was born November 4, 1831. Married to Anna Kreiner. They live in Manheim township, and are the parents of thirteen children: Mary K. (married to Samuel Behmer, Lancaster; family, Katie, Morris and another boy), David K. (deceased), Anna K. (married to Henry Adams; three children), John K. (married; family of three children), Amanda K. (married, having one child), Emma, Christian, Henry (married; family of one child), Abraham, Katie, Ella, Samuel, and Franklin.

Elizabeth F. Landis[4] was born November 30, 1833. Married to Cyrus Kitch, blacksmith, of this county. She died here, leaving a family of six children: Anna Catharine L. (married to George Brewen), Minnie L. (unmarried), Mary Lizzie L., Dora Eve L. (unmarried), Charles L., and Cyrus L. (unmarried).

Mary F. Landis was born July 18, 1837. Married to Samuel White, a moulder, of Lancaster city. Removed to Missouri. She has seven children: George L. (married; five children, four deceased), Anna L. (married to John Roadweiler; family, John and Flora), Willie L., Andrew, Samuel, Elsie, and Mary.

Daniel F. Landis was born December 6, 1840. Married to Elizabeth Hoffman, of Neffsville, Manheim township; she died, leaving one child. He married a second wife, Anna ———, who died with no issue. Daniel married a third wife, Eliza Leeds, who also died, leaving two children: Walter (married; has a family of one child) and Nettie. He finally married the fourth wife, Mary Ribble, with whom he has no children. He is a canal boatman, and resides at Havre-de-Grace, Md.

Hettie F. Landis[4] was born March 20, 1842. She was married to Elijah Frame, of Neffsville. They have one son, John L., a watchmaker. Both Hettie and her husband are now deceased.

Susanna F. Landis[4] was born December 6, 1846. Married to Albert Shissler, from the vicinity of Lampeter. He perished for want of food while a prisoner in the late war. Susanna was afterward married to Henry Bigot. Had two children, who since died; the mother is also deceased.

John F. Landis[4] was born January 2, 1851. Married to Sarah Ann Kuhns. They had four children: Margaret K., Susanna, Anna, and Sarah Ann. Mr. Landis is a bricklayer and resides in Lancaster city.

Sarah Ann Landis[4] was born April 7, 1854; deceased.

Mary S. Landis,[3] second daughter of John,[2] was born May 2, 1804. Married to Jacob Grossman (born September 4, 1804), on February 26, 1826. They resided near New Haven, Warwick township. Had eleven children, viz.: John L. (Warwick township), Jacob L. (deceased), George L. (Lancaster city), Henry L. (Plymouth, Ind.), Margaret L. (near Plymouth, Ind.), Andrew L. (deceased), David L. (emigrated to the West), Levi L. (Chester county), Catharine L. (Rohrerstown), and Daniel L. (near Lake Kettle, Plymouth, Ind).

David S. Landis,[3] second son of John,[2] was born in Manheim township, September 6, 1805. Married to Anna, daughter of John Frick, this county. They had ten children: First born (deceased), Eliza F., Mary, Ephraim, David, John, Abraham, Samuel, Fanny, and Margaret. Mr. Landis died December 25, 1863, aged 58 years, 3 months and 19 days. Anna, his wife (born August 28, 1808), died June 23, 1885; aged 76 years, 9 months and 25 days.

Eliza F. Landis was born January 28, 1829, in Manheim township. Married to George Y. Shreiner, of the same township, October 5, 1857. They reside at present in Lititz, this county. Are the parents of eight children: Sarah L. (East Cocalico township; five children), Franklin L. (East Hempfield township; eight children), David L. (Clay township; one child), Amanda L. (Drumore township; eight children), Eliza L. (West Donegal township; one son), Anna L. (deceased), Fanny L. (probably of Reading, Pa.; one son), and George L. (Lititz; one daughter).

Mary F. Landis[4] was born October 28, 1830. Died April 21, 1842; aged 11 years and 28 days.

Ephraim F. Landis was born January 10, 1833. Married to Sarah Weaver. He carried on cabinet-making at his father's place. Afterward moved to Petersburg, East Hempfield township; from thence he emigrated to the State of Ohio with his family. Had six children, viz.: Reuben W., Emma, Fanny, Elizabeth, Amanda, and Anna; the latter three are unmarried. Ephraim died in Akron, Ohio, presumably from heart disease; he dropped over dead, ten miles from home, having paid his fare to Wadsworth, where he then lived. His age was 53 years, 1 month and 5 days.

Reuben W. Landis[5] married Sarah Jane, daughter of Michael Acker. He was a blacksmith by occupation. No family.

Emma W. Landis[5] was married to David Eshleman, supposed to be a railroad repairman. They have three girls and one boy.

Fanny W. Landis[5] was married to Albert Roshorn. They have a family of three boys.

David F. Landis[4] was born July 4, 1835. Married to Mary Ressler (born in Warwick township, August 27, 1837). He was a carpenter by trade, at which he worked for some years in Bachman & Dehuff's planing mill, Columbia, till the spring of 1886. He accepted the foremanship in B. F. Hiestand's planing mill, Marietta, and moved there in the spring of 1887. Has two children: John R. and Susan R.

John R. Landis[5] was born June 2, 1857. Married Phoebe A. (born in Chanceford township, York county, March 28, 1858), daughter of John Depue, of Columbia. They have three children: Mazie D., born in Mountville, April 29, 1878; John D., born in Mountville, July 11, 1879; and David D., born in Columbia, May 20, 1882. John R. commenced railroading December 14, 1878, as brakeman; was promoted to flagman in 1884, on the Pennsylvania Railroad between Columbia and Philadelphia.

Susan R. Landis[5] was born October 27, 1858. Resides in Columbia, this county.

John F. Landis[4] was born September 30, 1837. Married to Magdalena G. (born December 6, 1839), daughter of Frederick Keller, of Penn township, this county, on September 13, 1859. Worked on his father's farm until spring of 1868. Then moved to Elizabeth township, this county, on the farm of the late Joseph Snyder, deceased, which he occupied until February 17, 1880. From there he moved to West Donegal township, this county, on the farm of his wife's uncle, John Gross, deceased. He has eleven children: Lizzie K., Franklin K., Martin K., Amanda K., Phares, Samuel, Maggie, John, Katie, Harry, and Clayton.

Lizzie K. Landis[5] was born July 25, 1860, in Elizabeth township. Married to Jacob W. Horst (born March 4, 1857), of Ephrata, this county, October 14, 1879. They have one son, Jacob L., born February 14, 1885.

Franklin K. Landis[5] was born November 9, 1861. Married to Amanda E. (born May 9, 1863), daughter of Rev. Peter Ebersole, of Conoy township, October 2, 1884. They are the parents of two children: Katie E., born June 18, 1885; and Clayton E., born July 16, 1886.

Martin K. Landis[5] was born March 1, 1863. Married to Lizzie (born June 18, 1858), daughter of Lewis Leicht, of Elizabethtown, on September 24, 1885. Occupies a small farm at Anchor, Mount Joy township, this county.

Amanda K. Landis[5] was born April 12, 1864. Died June 4, 1864, aged 1 month and 23 days.

Phares K. Landis[5] was born July 15, 1865. Married to Lizzie L., daughter of Jacob W. Heisey, of West Donegal township, this county, on November 13, 1886. She was born February 26, 1864. They occupy his father's farm, of the same township. No family.

Samuel K. Landis[5] was born May 19, 1867. Unmarried.

Magdalena K. Landis was born May 11, 1869. Unmarried.

John K. Landis was born November 18, 1871. Died May 6, 1872, aged 5 months and 18 days.

Katie K. Landis was born January 17, 1874. Unmarried.

Harry K. Landis was born March 11, 1875.

Clayton K. Landis was born September 2, 1878. Died January 22, 1885, aged 6 years, 4 months and 20 days.

Abraham F. Landis[4] was born December 7, 1839. Married to Sarah H. (born November 13, 1840), daughter of David Brubaker, Warwick township, this county, on October 2, 1860. After residing ten years in that township, they emigrated to Washington county, Md., in 1870, settling in the 13th District of said county, seven miles north-west of Hagerstown. They have five children: David B., born December 24, 1862; Samuel and John B., twins, born April 21,

1871 (John died at the age of 6 hours, and Samuel at the age of 16 days); Anna B., born May 12, 1872; and Lizzie B., born August 8, 1877.

Samuel F. Landis[4] was born May 3, 1842. He lived with his father in Manheim township, near Neffsville, where he took typhoid fever and died, single, October 21, 1865, aged 23 years, 5 months and 18 days.

Fanny F. Landis[4] was born October 1, 1844. She was married to Jacob Kurtz, of near Ephrata, this county. They lived with his brother on his father's farm a little over a year, when they separated and she returned to her mother's home. Shortly after she took typhoid fever and died August 24, 1865, aged 20 years, 10 months and 23 days. Departed without family.

Margaret F. Landis[4] was born February 27, 1848. Married to Christian M. (born June 26, 1847), son of Samuel Hess, of Manheim township, this county, in 1867. His occupation is farming near Neffsville. They have no family.

Margaretta S. Landis,[3] third daughter of John,[2] was born June 18, 1807. Married to Daniel Geib (born September 12, 1805), on December 26, 1826. His occupation was farming about one and a-half miles east of Oregon, Manheim township, this county, until his death, June 2, 1848, aged 43 years, 8 months and 20 days. She then returned to her parents' home, where she lived until their death. Margaretta had five children: David L., born March 12, 1828 (deceased); John L., born December 17, 1830 (married); Anna L., born May 1, 1832 (married); Samuel, born October 12, 1834; and Margaret, born January 10, 1837 (married).

Anna S. Landis,[3] fourth daughter of John,[2] was born December 4, 1807. Married to Peter Grube, of this county. They had five children: Margaret L., born November 14, 1828; Elizabeth L. (married); Leah L., born March 8, 1833; David, born May 4, 1838; and Peter, born May 12, 1840. Mr. Grube died in the State of Ohio. After Peter's death, Anna S. was again married to Josiah Snyder. They occupy a farm near Johnson's Corner, Summit county, Ohio, and had three children: John L., born in 1843; Anna L., born November 10, 1844; and an infant son, deceased.

Jacob S. Landis,[3] third son of John,[2] was born in this county, February 18, 1810. Married to Mary A. Miller (born December 10, 1811), on September 28, 1830. They emigrated to Ohio and settled near Shelby, Richland county, in March, 1837. His occupation was farming; he also preached the Gospel about 35 years and was a faithful minister. Had ten children, as follows: Mary Ann M., Leah, Amanda, John, Jacob, Isaac, Margaret, Catharine, Susan, and David. Jacob S. died March 3, 1874, aged 64 years, 1 month and 5 days.

Mary Ann M. Landis,[4] oldest daughter, was born in Lancaster county, December 11, 1831. Married to Jacob Kunkleman, Shelby, Ohio, on August 28, 1851. Mr. Kunkleman was a farmer by occupation, and emigrated to Allen county, that State, in April, 1864. They are the parents of thirteen children, viz.: Lucinda B., born May 31, 1852 (Beaver Dam, O.); Mary C., born Oct. 9, 1853 (school teacher); Amanda E., born January 2, 1855 (Cranberry, O.); John William, born October 23, 1856 (Newton, Harvey county, Kansas); Maggie A., born February 7, 1858 (Lima, O.); Benjamin Franklin, born October 6, 1859 (farmer); Rebecca J., born July 4, 1861; Daniel Iden, born February 26, 1863 (Newton, Kan.); Isaac, born March 4, 1865 (deceased); Roccelina E., born November 23, 1866 (dressmaker); Oliver Ulysses, born January 27, 1869 (attending school); Edith A., born May 2, 1871; and Leah Adela M., born February 15, 1874.

Leah M. Landis[4] was born near Shelby, Richland county, Ohio, April 28, 1833. Married to John Stover (born May 23, 1823), February 10, 1853. They are the parents of five children: Mary A., born February 16, 1854 (deceased); Nancy C., born March 31, 1857 (married; has one son); Elizabeth L., born November 20, 1859 (married; three children); Henry F., born November 14, 1862 (married; one daughter); and Edwin J., born January 9, 1865 (deceased). Mr. Stover has been in a helpless condition for about five years past. He quit farming for about three years, and the children live on his farm near Shelby, Richland county, Ohio.

John M. Landis[4] was born in Richland county, Ohio, November 16, 1837. Married to Mary A. Finicle (born March 16, 1839), December 28, 1857. Their occupation is farming. Children: David D., Warie I., Orville F., and Lester J.

David D. Landis[5] was born September 18, 1859. Married to Etta Bear (born January 21, 1866), of Greensburg, Ohio, December 17, 1885. They have one daughter: Verna A., born September 1, 1886. David is in the hardware business at Shelby, Ohio.

Warie I. Landis[5] was born April 20, 1862. He is a farmer by occupation. Married to Mary I. Wentz (born November 9, 1862), of Shelby, Ohio, December 25, 1884. They are the parents of one child, Lester L., born November 25, 1885.

Orville F. Landis[5] was born February 3, 1864. Follows farming at Shelby, Ohio.

Lester J. Landis,[5] fourth son of John M., was born August 16, 1869.

Jacob M. Landis,[4] son of Jacob S., was born December 29, 1839. He was a member of the 64th Ohio Volunteer Infantry, in the war of the Rebellion. Died at Bowling Green, Kentucky, November, 1862, aged 22 years and some months.

Isaac M. Landis[4] was born in Richland county, Ohio, October 9, 1842. He lived with his father on the farm till nineteen years of age, when he enlisted in Company C., 20th Ohio Volunteer Infantry. Served about one year, and, also, shared in the Vicksburg campaign. Came home again and farmed two years, after which he sold out and went into the hardware business at New London, Ohio. After being five years in this line of trade, he sold out again and entered a saw-mill near Carey, Ohio; there he sawed four years. After selling out once again he bought a saw-mill at Tiffin, Ohio, and moved it to Bascom, that State, where he sawed for a period of two years. Disposing of the saw mill, he moved on a farm near Shelby, Ohio, where he now resides. He was married to Miss Ellen Finicle, December 22, 1864. They have two children: Carrie Ellen F., born February 5, 1866 (music teacher), and Zuleika Olive, born October 30, 1867. The latter is an expert violinist.

Margaret M. Landis[4] was born July 16, 1845, in Shelby, Ohio. Married to William S. McDowell (born August 7, 1834), December 26, 1862. They are the parents of six children: Irma, born October 1, 1863 (deceased); Orles, born November 26, 1864; Trella, born September 20, 1866; Elvina, born December 6, 1869; Edma, born October 24, 1872; and

Effie, born April 5, 1875. The two latter children were born on a farm at Maxinkuckee, Marshall county, Indiana, where the parents had removed from Shelby. Margaret died at the age of 29 years, 8 months and 17 days. Mr. McD. died at Ashland, Oregon, July 28, 1876.

Catharine M. Landis[4] was born December 12, 1850. Married to Thomas A. Cline (born January 29, 1849), November 19, 1868. Farming at Warsaw, Indiana, since April 6, 1876. Had nine children, born in different places: Dora B., born July 14, 1870; Trella M., born November 17, 1871; infant son, born February 1, 1873; Marion L., born September 24, 1874 (deceased); Albert B., born November 26, 1875 (deceased); Urey L., born June 17, 1878; Frankie D., born September 20, 1880; Carl C., born May 6, 1882 (deceased); and infant son, born April 6, 1883.

David M. Landis,[4] son of Jacob S., was born August 21, 1856. Died September 25, 1856, aged 1 month and 4 days.

Henry S. Landis,[3] fourth son of John,[2] was born in Lancaster county, June 28, 1811. Married to Susan Miller (born May 3, 1811), probably of Lampeter, this county, February 23, 1832. They were the parents of thirteen children, viz.: Margaret M., Susan M., Mary M., John M., Henry M., Anna M., David M., Elizabeth M., Sarah M., Martha M., Jacob M., Daniel M., and Isaac M. The parents last resided at Petersburg, this county, where Henry S. died March 27, 1883, aged 65 years and 24 days.

Margaret M. Landis[4] was born September 11, 1833. Married to John Christ, in 1850. He died in August, 1879.

Susanna M. Landis[4] was born September 10, 1835. Died September 25, 1854, aged 19 years and 15 days.

Mary M. Landis[4] was born July 19, 1837. Married to Daniel Roether (born June 28, 1825), of this county, December 5, 1861. They were formerly ‧ residents of the Farmersville hotel, West Earl township, but now occupy a farm in Ephrata township, this county. They have nine children: Elizabeth L., born November 11, 1862; John L., born June 13, 1864; Henry, born September 2, 1865; William, born September 26, 1867; Sarah, born May 12, 1869; Anna, born March 7, 1872; Emma, born January 9, 1875; Rufus, born March 27, 1877; and Lillie, born January 4, 1879.

John M. Landis[4] was born January 8, 1839. Married to Mary A. Buch (born October 2, 1847), of Manheim township, this county, in 1877. They have nine children: Florence B., born November 30, 1877 (died December 14, 1877, aged 14 days); Elmer B., born October 4, 1878; Scott B., born September 9, '79 (died October 21, '79, aged 1 month and 12 days); Clara, born April 11, '81; Nora, born April 4, '82 (died May 2, '82, aged 28 days); John, born June 9, '83 (died October 11, '83, aged 4 months and 2 days); Lizzie, born May 1, '85; Gabriel, born May 13, '86 (died September 8, '86, aged 3 months and 25 days); and Martin, born June 24, '87 (died August 16, '87, aged 1 month and 23 days.

Henry M. Landis,[4] son of Henry S., was born July 5, 1840.

Anna M. Landis[4] was born October 25, 1841. Married to Abraham R. Young (born February 15, 1841). He is a mason by occupation, and lives in East Petersburg, this county. They are the parents of eight children: Sarah L., born August 7, 1864 (married); Martha L., born September 23, 1866 (deceased); Mary L., born July 14, 1868 (married); Katie L., born August 25, 1872; Landis L., born June 7, 1874; Lizzie L., born November 14, 1878; Abraham L., and Earl L., born August 14, 1886.

David M. Landis[4] was born December 4, 1842. Married to Rebecca D. Lupold (born March 8, 1858), probably of East Petersburg, this county. They have four children, as follows: Anna L., born February 2, 1878; Phares, born July 3, 1883; and David, born August 18, 1886. David M. is a farmer.

Elizabeth M. Landis[4] was born October 20, 1844. Married to Samuel Bemesderfer, East Petersburg, this county. They resided there until she died of consumption, May 7, 1884, aged 39 years, 6 months and 17 days.

Sarah M. Landis[4] was born August 21, 1846. Married to Hiram D. Bishop (born April 16, 1844). Sarah died, without issue, in East Petersburg, March 18, 1878, aged 31 years, 6 months and 27 days. Mr. B. died April 25, 1879, aged 35 years and 9 days.

Martha M. Landis[4] was born June 2, 1848. Married to H. W. Graybill, of East Petersburg, in 186–. Had one daughter,

Cora M., born July 14, 1868 (deceased). Martha died August 2, 1868, aged 20 years and 2 months.

Jacob M. Landis, son of Henry S., was born November 7, 1850. Unmarried.

Daniel M. Landis was born January 20, 1852. He is a laborer by occupation. Married to Anna Forice (born November 22, 1863). They had three sons: Harvey F., born July 19, '83 (died July 30, '85, aged 2 years and 11 days); Albert F., born September 8, '85; and Willie F., born August 17, '86.

Isaac M. Landis[4] was born August 10, 1855. Married to Lizzie Dussinger (born May 30, 1860), February 16, 1882. They are residents of East Petersburg. No family.

Leah S. Landis,[3] fifth daughter of John E., was born near Neffsville, this county, February 27, 1813. Married to Daniel Grube (born November 27, 1812), of this county, January 12, 1836. After their marriage they emigrated to Ohio, and about 1840 moved to Marion township, Allen county, Indiana, where they bought a farm and settled for the remainder of their lives. They were the parents of six children, viz.: Israel L., born December 1, 1836 (lives near Warsaw, Ind.); Lavinia L., born July 13, 1839 (deceased); Sarah Ann L., born June 26, 1842 (married); Daniel L., born September 19, 1844 (unmarried); John L., born January 26, 1847 (deceased); and Margaret L., born October 25, 1850 (married). Mr. and Mrs. Grube were pious people, and it is said, gave the free use for years of their farm house as a place of worship for the Church of God denomination. Leah died December 18, 1878, aged 65 years, 10 months and 11 days. Mr. Grube died December 28, 1863, aged 51 years, 1 month and 1 day.

Magdalena S. Landis,[3] the sixth daughter of John,[2] was born April 3, 1814. Died in Lancaster county, August 27, 1814, aged 4 months and 24 days.

Susanna S. Landis,[3] seventh daughter of John,[2] was born in this county, September 14, 1815. Married to John Burkholder (born August 24, 1841), March 13, 1838. They reside in Warwick township, and have four children: Sarah L., born July 23, 1841; Gabriel L., born July 27, 1843 (deceased); Isaac L., born September 18, 1846 (deceased); and Magdalena L. (married).

LINEAL DESCENDANTS OF JOHN,[1] OF DAUPHIN.

In the Eighteenth century, about 1775, John Landis,[1] a young man, with his bachelor brother, and a sister (who was since married to a man named Nolt), came to this country and settled in Dauphin county. John had at least five sons: Henry, Christian, Benjamin, Abraham, and Jacob. One daughter married Benjamin Johnson, and the other became the wife of the late Sheriff Huber. John lived, also, at one time in Manheim township, Lancaster county. Some of the children moved to this county, among them Christian.

Christian Landis[2] was married to Susan Brubaker, of Rohrerstown. They lived at Roseville, where Mr. Landis began the business of coachmaking about 1824, which he carried on there until his death. His children were: Abraham B., Jacob B., and Anna (Mrs. Samuel Kohr, Rockford, Ill.)

Abraham B. Landis[3] learned the coachmaking trade with his father, whom he succeeded in 1843. He removed to Mount Joy, in 1858, where he established the Landis Coach Works. This industrial establishment has had a large Southern trade. Mr. Landis was one of the organizers of the Friendship Fire Company, of Mount Joy, on January 27, 1868. He married Maria Summy. They have no children.

Jacob B. Landis,[3] coachmaker, was married to Fanny K. Long, near Landisville. Their children were: Benjamin L., Samuel K., Jacob F., Aaron, Abraham, and Ellen, the latter three now deceased.

Benjamin L. Landis[4] was married to Emma Busser, of near Brickerville. He was a coachmaker by trade; but is now living in Rapho township, and makes cigar boxes in Landisville. His children are: Virginia, Ella, Benjamin, Edwin, Abraham, and Dolly.

Samuel K. Landis[4] was married to Susan M. Swartley, Landisville. They had seven children, five of whom are living: Eva, Mary, Walter, Fannie, Harry (Abraham and Granville, twins, deceased). Samuel is a cigarmaker. •

Jacob F. Landis[4] was born April 6, 1860. He finished his education at Millersville, after which he taught school. For the past two years he has been in Kansas, and was recently located at Abilene, that State. He is unmarried. His mother lives at Landisville.

"Schmidt" Jacob Landis,[2] a son of John Landis, of Dauphin county, moved to Lancaster county and settled at Landis Valley, where he carried on blacksmithing. He married Elizabeth Kauffman. They had four children: John, Jacob, Nancy, and Elizabeth.

John Landis[3] was an edge-tool manufacturer. He was rather "wild" in his young days, and was known as "Devil" John. He died, however, to his credit, a temperate man.

"Smith" Jacob Landis, jr.,[3] son of the elder Jacob, was born at Landis Valley, in 1813. He was married to Catharine Grabill (who now lives on North Queen street, Lancaster). Their children are: Abram G., Adam (Lancaster), Lizzie (Lancaster), and Grabill (Dodge City, Kansas). "Smith" Jacob was the founder and first Postmaster of Landis Valley, where he died in 1861. (See Part IV.)

Abram Grabill Landis[4] was born in 1842. He was married to Ellie F. Hubley, in 1873. Their children are: Nevin, Maud, May, and Paul, the first-named being deceased. Abram moved from this county to Kansas, in 1870, and he is yet there in the town of Sterling. He was engaged in general merchandise, milling and banking; subsequently in banking exclusively, until 1884, when he sold out and is now loaning money privately.

JOHN A. LANDIS, OF BERKS.

John A. Landis was born September 15, 1777, and came to Lancaster county from Berks. He was twice married: 1. Beitler; 2. Sarah Bubb (died October 3, 1874, aged 75 years, 10 months and 30 days). Mr. Landis and a relative of his first wife opened the first theatrical and circus building in Lancaster city, in a large structure erected for the purpose, on West Orange street.* The Western hotel was opened by him at the sign of "The Wagon," corner of West Orange and Water streets, Lancaster, in June, 1814. In 1819 Landis

---

*The walls of the "Circus" building afterward weakened, and while the place was being torn down it is said Landis, who was standing on a wall at the time, took several somersaults from it without injury to himself, thus adding to his fame as an athlete.

opened the first museum in the city, opposite the "Circus" building. It was called the Lancaster Museum, but better known as the Landis Museum.* Some time afterward it was removed to the building that formerly stood where the present *Examiner* printing office is located. Mr. Landis next removed to where Haberbush & Son now keep a saddlery on Penn Square, where the Museum flourished for many years and became widely known. The last removal of the Landis' Museum was made in 1836 or '37 to the Rohrer House, corner of West Chestnut and North Queen streets. In 1838 Mr. Landis sold the curiosities to Westhaeffer & Getz.† The Museum was a wonderful attraction in its time, and many people yet tell of the success Landis made of it. He was no mean genius, but his ingenuity never brought him riches. He died, leaving no children, March 8, 1862, and his body rests beneath a monument bearing the Masonic emblem, in Shreiner's cemetery, Lancaster.

DESCENDANTS OF ELIAS, OF MONTGOMERY.

Elias Landis lived and died in Montgomery county, this State. He was married to Mary Funk. Their children were: Isaac, Dilman, John, Jacob, and Henry. The former three never married.

Jacob Landis² was married and had the following children: Jacob, John, Elias, Daniel, Joseph, Isaac, Christian, Catharine, Mary, Susan, Elizabeth, and Sarah.

Henry Landis² was married to Susan Detweiler. They had nine children: Jacob, Henry, Elias, Joseph, Elizabeth, Mary, Sarah, Susan, and Anna. All of these were unmarried except Elias and Joseph; and all are now deceased except Susan and Joseph. Henry² died in Montgomery county, at the age of 52 years. Shortly after his death his

---

*In an advertisement dated October 23, 1819, Mr. Landis informed the public that he had collected a large number of natural and artificial curiosities. These were ready for the public on December 4 of that year. The admission was fixed "at the low rate of 25 cents," and the Museum would remain open every day (Sundays excepted), "from 9 o'clock in the morning until sunset."

†Charles S. Getz sold the collection to Wood & Peale, of Philadelphia, who took it to Cincinnati, where, unfortunately, all the curiosities were destroyed by fire about 1850.

widow and her children removed to Lancaster county and settled in West Lampeter township, near Lampeter Square.

Elias Landis[3] was twice married. He had two sons, Henry
and Jacob, both of whom served in the army. Jacob is married and lives in Missouri.

Joseph Landis[3] was born in 1818. Married, in 1856, to
Esther Krug (born 1825; died 1886). Their children were:
Daniel K. and Benjamin K. Resided near Lampeter Square,
being occupied with farming, and moved to Strasburg about
fourteen years ago.

Daniel K. Landis[4]* was born April 28, 1858. He is now
successfully conducting one of the largest general stores in
Strasburg, this county. He was Treasurer of that borough
in 1882–3; and is unmarried.

Benjamin K. Landis[4] was born August 3, 1859. He was
engaged at storekeeping until his death, at the age of 22.
Unmarried.

BENJAMIN AND JOHN, OF MONTGOMERY.

Benjamin Landis, of Montgomery county, had six children:
Elizabeth, Magdalena, Jacob D., Benjamin, Sarah, and Mary.
Benjamin[1] died in 1842.

Jacob D. Landis[2] was born in Montgomery county, July 18,
1834. Removed when young to Safe Harbor, Lancaster
county; went next to Millersville; then to Slackwater, where
he was married to Elizabeth Conrad. Lived at New Danville
from 1860 to 1880 (part of which time he served in the war;
see Part III). For the past seven years Jacob has resided in
Lancaster city, where he is interested in tobacco. His children are: B. Franklin, Mary C. (Volrath), Sarah A. (Breneman), Jacob H. (married to a Shubrooks), Lizzie A., Emma
F., and Elvina.

Benjamin's[1] brothers and sisters were: John, Isaac, Polly,
Lydia, Lizzie (died 1877), and Sarah.

"Schoolmaster" John Landis, brother of Benjamin,[1] lived
at Indiantown, Manor township, this county, and married

---

*D. K. Landis' great-great-grandfather Krug emigrated from Germany
to America when quite young and married a woman of this county
named Herr, who lived and died here.

Rebecca Stauffer. Their children were: Lizzie (Seitz), Susan (died, aged about 5 years), Sarah (Hiller, Columbia), Mary (married to Martin Kendig, Lancaster), John (married to Martha Miller), Barbara (Urban), Magdalena (deceased), Lydia (Stanley, Columbia), Jacob (served in the war; afterward resided in California), and Adeline (Fridy, Mountville).

JOHN LANDES, OF MONTGOMERY.

John Landes,[1]* of Montgomery county, had five sons and five daughters, viz.: Abraham, John S., George, Mary, Annie, Henry, Peggy, Lizzie (deceased), Jacob, and Lydia.

John S. Landes,[2] second son, was the only one of the family to come to Lancaster county. He is married and has three children: Amanda, John E. and William G. John S. is interested in patent-rights, and has a residence at No. 544 East Orange street, Lancaster.

Amanda Landes,[3] oldest child of John S., is well known as an elocutionary reader. She is at present a member of the faculty in Millersville State Normal School.

John E. Landes is a cabinet-maker, in the city of Lancaster.

William G. Landes, a watch-maker, removed some time since to Peoria, Illinois.

---

* All of this family invariably write their name *Landes*.

PART III.

LANDIS SOLDIERS OF THE REBELLION.

A COMPLETE LIST OF MEN WHO SERVED THE UNION
FAITHFULLY AND HONORABLY — WHEN THEY WERE
MUSTERED IN, PROMOTED AND FINALLY DISCHARGED.

IN the War of the Rebellion a number of male members
of the Landis family of this county entered service, and
bravely fought for the preservation of the national
Union. It is a source of much gratification to the Historian
to present herewith a complete record* of these soldiers:

Abram G. Landis, 2d Lieutenant Co. K, 195th Regiment; 1
year's service. Mustered in, March 2, 1865; mustered out
with Company, January 31, 1866.

Abraham G. Landis, Private Co. H, 47th Regiment, Militia
of 1863. Mustered in, July 9, 1863; discharged, August 16,
1863.

Benjamin F. Landis, Private Independent Battery I; 6
months' service. Mustered in, June 30, 1863; mustered out
with Battery, January 7, 1864.

Benjamin F. Landis, 2d Lieutenant Co. H, 203d Regiment;
1 year's service. Mustered in, September 5, 1864; promoted
from Sergeant, March 1, 1865; mustered out with Company,
June 22, 1865.

Christian Landis, Private Co. F (Emergency Troops), 50th
Regiment, Militia of 1863. Mustered in July 8, 1863; discharged, August 15, 1863.

Daniel F. Landis, Private Co. B, 79th Regiment; 3 years'
service. Mustered in, September 27, 1861; discharged on
Surgeon's certificate.

* Aided by a careful research made by Mr. Eli B. Landis.

David Landis, Private Co. A, 12th Regiment, Militia of 1862. Mustered in, September 11, 1862; discharged, September 12, 1862.

David Landis, Private Co. F, 50th Regiment, Militia of 1863. Mustered in, July 8, 1863; discharged, August 15, 1863.

David M. Landis, Private Co. H, 47th Regiment, Militia of 1863. Mustered in, July 9, 1863; discharged, August 14, 1863.

Eli Landis, Private Co. F, 50th Regiment, Militia of 1863 (Emergency Troops). Mustered in, July 8, 1863; discharged, August 15, 1863.

Emanuel Landis, Private Co. K, 178th Regiment, drafted Militia; 9 months' service. Mustered in, November 4, 1862; mustered out with Company, July 27, 1863.

Emanuel G. Landis, Corporal Co. D, 195th Regiment; 1 year's service. Mustered in, February 14, 1865; mustered out with Company, January 31, 1866.

Henry Landis, Private Co. A, 99th Regiment; 3 years' service. Mustered in, July 26, 1861; wounded at Gettysburg, Pa., July 2, 1863, and Spottsylvania C. H., Va., May 12, 1864; transferred to Veteran Reserve Corps, date unknown.

Henry M. Landis, Private Independent Battery I; 3 years' service. Mustered in, January 9, 1864; mustered out with Battery, June 23, 1865.

Henry W. Landis, Private Co. I, 195th Regiment; 100 days' service. Mustered in, July 21, 1864; mustered out with Company, November 4, 1864.

Israel S. Landis, Private Co. H, 47th Regiment, Militia of 1863. Mustered in, July 9, 1863; discharged, August 14, 1863.

Jacob D. Landis, Private Co. B, 79th Regiment; 3 years' service. Mustered in, September 7, 1861; discharged, October 3, 1864, expiration of term.

Jacob R. Landis, Private Independent Battery I; 3 years' service. Mustered in, January 21, 1864; mustered out with Battery, June 23, 1865.

Jacob S. Landis, Private Co. F, 50th Regiment, Militia of 1863 (Emergency Troops). Mustered in, July 8, 1863; discharged, August 15, 1863.

John B. Landis, Private Co. G, 92d Regiment, Ninth Cavalry; 3 years' service. Mustered in, August 17, 1864, for 1 year; died at New York, June 26,* 1865; buried in Cypress Hill Cemetery, Long Island.

John G. Landis, Private Co. F, 50th Regiment, Militia of 1863 (Emergency Troops). Mustered in, July 8, 1863; discharged, August 15, 1863.

John K. Landis, Sergeant Co. E, 135th Regiment; 9 months' service. Mustered in, August 11, 1862; promoted from Corporal, April 16, 1863; mustered out with Company, May 24, 1863.

John K. Landis, Captain Co. C, 197th Regiment; 100 days' service. Mustered in, July 15, 1864; mustered out with Company, November 11, 1864.

Monroe Landis, Private Co. C, 162d Regiment, 17th Cavalry; 3 years' service. Mustered in, August 20, 1864; mustered out with Company, June 16, 1865.

Samuel Landis, Private Co. H, 135th Regiment; 9 months' service. Mustered in, August 12, 1862; discharged, December 26, 1862.

Samuel Landis, Private Independent Battery I; 3 years' service. Mustered in, January 2, 1864; mustered out with Battery, June 23, 1865.

Samuel S. Landis, Private Co. F, 195th Regiment; 1 year's service. Mustered in, February (or March) 25, 1865; mustered out with Company, January 31, 1866.

---

* Burial record, June 22, 1865.

PART IV.

LANDISVILLE AND LANDIS VALLEY.

Two Villages of the County Founded by Landises—
Their Start and Subsequent Growth—Moral and
Spiritual Institutions—Industries, etc.

THE earlier, and later, growth of Landisville has been
but meagrely treated of in the past, historically speak-
ing; and it is with no little difficulty that the present
Historian has procured reliable material for this sketch. In
1798 Jacob Minnich erected the first house in the eastern part
of what is now Landisville. In 1808 Mr. Minnich built a
two-story hotel on the north side of the Lancaster and Elizabethtown turnpike, about six and one-half miles west of Lancaster. The following year his brother-in-law, Jacob Charles,
purchased a piece of ground from him, upon which he erected
a dwelling house and a blacksmith shop. It was in the same
year that Mr. Minnich also put up a large distillery. Prior
to 1825 several more dwellings were added to the first mentioned.

Centreville—Landisville.—In the fall of 1828 John Landis,
who owned a farm south-west of the tavern, purchased the
dwelling house* built by Mr. Charles and established a store
in it the following spring. Mr. Landis saw the necessity of
naming the little settlement, which began to assume the dig-
nity of a village, as a few more houses were built soon afterward. With the aid of his son, John C., a surveyor, Mr.
Landis laid out the village about that time and named it
"Centreville," from the fact that it was just equa-distant between Lancaster and Mount Joy. Several years thereafter,
about 1832, John Landis applied to the Post-Office Depart-

---

* Now occupied by Frederick Metzger, confectioner.

ment for a post-office, which was then established with him as first Postmaster. As there was already a Centreville office in Centre county, the Department took the liberty of naming the place "Landisville," which name it has kept since.

Its Postmasters.—The post-office at Landisville was at one time removed from Landis' store to a point near the present Reformed Mennonite meeting-house, then known as Snyder's store (now occupied by John M. Gochnauer). As S. S. Snyder, who became Postmaster, was also a Justice of the Peace, the office remained at his place a very short time and Mr. Landis got it back again. John C. Landis also served as Postmaster for some years until his death in 1854, when Jacob K. Minnich was appointed, with Israel C. Landis as assistant. Martin M. Swarr afterward kept the office at his store. Jacob K. Kurtz became the next Postmaster, after which Simon Minnich, sr., held the office until shortly before his death, with Henry E. Minnich as assistant. Daniel K. Wolf, upon being appointed, removed the office to his residence. Since 188-, John B. Kern has been Postmaster, with quarters at his shoe shop.

Places of Worship.—The Old Mennonites erected a log meeting-house* at what is now Landisville, about the year 1790. In 1855 a brick house was built near by, to which an addition was put a score of years since, the interior being also remodeled. The large room has a seating capacity of five hundred persons. Meetings are held there every four weeks, with an afternoon Sunday-school during the summer months. The present ministers are: Jacob N. Brubacher (Bishop), John B. Landis and Tobias Shenk.

About 1840, the Church of God was organized at Landisville, its services for a time being held at private houses. Jacob H. Hershey, now living at Rohrerstown, was one of its first members, as was, also, John C. Landis, now deceased, and others. In 1843, a frame house of worship was erected which is still standing, although improved since internally. It has seating room for about two hundred souls. During the winter of 1887-8 the same edifice was enlarged and considerably im-

---

* Yet standing; occupied by Benjamin Brown.

proved. A flourishing Sabbath-school is held in the same building. The present pastor is Rev. F. L. Nicodemus.

The Reformed Mennonites first held services in the Bethel. They erected a brick structure* east of the village, in 1869. It has about two hundred and fifty sittings. Meetings every four weeks, with occasional evening services. The regular ministers are: Abraham Long, Martin Musser and Levi Shenk. John Kohr, sr. (deceased), was Bishop until his death.

Camp-Meetings.—Over forty years ago, what may be termed a type of "religious insanity" broke out south of Landisville, in an encampment under the charge of Second Adventists or "Millerites." An extended account of the odd affair was printed in the Landisville *Vigil*, Vol. I., No. 15.

About 1870 the Landisville Camp-meeting Association was formed, and a tract of woodland lying close to the village was bought from Dr. Andrew Kauffman. This grove was tastefully fitted up and since improved with cottages and suitable buildings. Up to date seventeen annual meetings have been held there. Methodists from Harrisburg, Reading, Columbia, Lancaster, etc., worship there.

Musical and Literary.—On September 4, 1858, the "Mechanicks Band of Landisville"† was organized, with these officers: W. D. Reitzel, president; E. D. Golden, vice president; Emanuel Newcomer, secretary; J. B. Kern, treasurer. Twelve members composed the full band: W. D. Reitzel, G. W. Sener, Emanuel Newcomer, C. H. Newcomer, Jacob Souders, J. B. Kern, J. J. Golden, E. D. Golden, I. C. Landis, Solomon Seamer, Reuben Pickel, and Daniel Kern. Three other names appear on the roll of membership: Joseph Musselman, Daniel M. Brown and Christian H. Mayer. War breaking out, the Band disbanded about 1863, after flourishing several years.

In 1886 a small musical club, known as the Landisville Orchestra, had a brief existence.

A couple of literary societies assembled at Landisville in the past, the best known of which was in existence from the

---

*The building committee was composed of Messrs. John K. Long, Benjamin K. Long and Jacob S. Trout.

†From secretary's book in possession of Israel C. Landis.

winter of 1881 to the spring of '84. The Landisville Literary Society met every Friday evening and held very successful meetings.

In 1882 the Union Temperance Society was started, which existed until the summer of '86.

The old public school building, between the Bethel and Old Mennonite churches, was torn down several years before the national Centennial; and since then two graded, brick buildings near by were erected for school purposes.

Industries.—The largest industrial establishment in the place is Simon B. Minnich's machine shop and wood-turning works, erected in 1883, and now under the management of the Landisville Manufacturing Company (Limited). The village has, in addition, two hotels, two general stores, one shoe shop, one tailor shop, two blacksmith shops, one coal and lumber yard, one tobacco warehouse, one chopping mill, one tin shop, one cigar-box factory, one cigar factory, one bakery, two confectionery stores, one carpenter shop, two slaughter houses, one carpet weaver, one furniture store and undertaker, one creamery, one cooper, etc., embracing all-told 28 or 30 business and professional establishments.

Mineral and Earth Deposits.—During the time of the Mexican War, Samuel Pickel (now deceased), while making a fence near Snapper creek, one and a-half miles east of Landisville, discovered lead ore. Soon afterward oxide of zinc was manufactured there for a brief time. About 1871 the mineral deposit was purchased by Bamford Brothers, of England, and extensive works built there for smelting zinc. These were operated until the fall of 1877. Since then, in 1883, the Lehigh Zinc & Iron Company leased the mines* for ten years; this company only used the works six months, and they are now idle.

A brick-yard was opened north-east of Landisville, in 1842, by Joseph G. Greider's father. About 1855 Joseph started in the business and carried on the yard successfully until after the war. The land of M. B. Landis is also suitable for making brick.

---

*A complete account of this mineral deposit and its discovery was published in the Lancaster *Inquirer*, November 20, 1886.

In 1870 Jacob S. Trout discovered a valuable bed of fire sand in East Hempfield township, south of Landisville. This sand is yet regularly shipped to some steel works from the village station.

Notable Fires.—The village has had several destructive fires, the most notable of which occurred during the summer of 1871, when Simon Minnich's hotel and store, two large frame buildings, were entirely consumed. A large three-story brick structure was afterward built at the same spot, in which Jacob B. Minnich now keeps a general store and the Sycamore House.

In 1881 an incendiary caused J. M. Rutt's new cigar factory and stable to be entirely consumed by fire.

During a thunder shower in 1885, a bolt of lightning entered the combined stable and workshop of J. C. Stewart, carpenter. The building was burnt to the ground, and a driving horse was lost in the flames.

Growth of the Village.—Up to about the death of Christian Hiestand, in the summer of 1877, Landisville grew slowly. Previous to that time two railroads, the Pennsylvania and Reading & Columbia had laid their tracks through the place, but the hamlet still remained toward the east of the "Crossing." In the past decade of years the growth of the village has been rapid, many fine residences being put up between the station and the old settlement. Most of these are occupied by retired farmers. The population to-day exceeds 450, and the number of dwelling houses is at this time 81.

LANDIS VALLEY.

"Smith" Jacob Landis was the founder of Landis Valley, a little settlement on the Lancaster & Ephrata turnpike, about four miles from the city of Lancaster.

In 1855 Jacob Landis built the hotel and kept it until his death in 1861, when the property was purchased by Isaac Landis. Jacob also obtained a post-office for the place prior to 1860, after whom it was named. It is said that this office was the outgrowth of one formerly located at Roseville.

H. L. Brackbill (once proprietor of the Landis Valley hotel) was Postmaster for a number of years. He was succeeded

by L. H. Longenecker. The office is at present in charge of
Mrs. Hannah A. Hauck, who received her appointment as
Postmistress at the close of 1887.

Wallace L. Hauck, one of the latest proprietors of the
Valley hotel, died November 27, 1887.

The settlement contains among its business establishments,
wagon and blacksmith shops, cigar manufactory, etc.

The Landis Valley Mennonite meeting-house is only a
short distance from the village.

PART V.

DIRECTORY OF LIVING ADULTS.

A COMPLETE LIST OF THE LANDIS FAMILY IN LANCASTER COUNTY, PA., WITH THEIR OCCUPATION AND POST-OFFICE ADDRESS, CLASSIFIED BY TOWNSHIPS, ALPHABETICALLY ARRANGED.

FOR the convenience of those who may desire a fairly complete list of names of the Landis people, for reference, the following useful directory is given herewith. It embraces all adults named Landis who now reside in the county of Lancaster:

ADAMSTOWN BOROUGH.

Benedict B., butcher, - Main street, near Broad.
David, merchant, - - Main street, near Broad.
Jacob, hatter, - Main street, near Lancaster road.

CLAY TOWNSHIP.

John B., laborer, - - - - Lincoln.
Reuben H., laborer, - - - Lincoln.

COCALICO (EAST) TOWNSHIP.

L. L., merchant, - - - - -
Monroe B., stone cutter, - - - Reamstown.

COLERAINE TOWNSHIP.

J. Frank, farmer, - - - - -

COLUMBIA BOROUGH.

David, carpenter, - - - 453 Manor street.

CONOY TOWNSHIP.

Benjamin, laborer,	Falmouth.
Henry E., farmer,	Bainbridge.
Henry R., laborer,	Falmouth.
Jacob E., farmer,	Bainbridge.
John E., farmer,	Bainbridge.
Joseph, farmer,	Falmouth.
Samuel R., laborer,	Bainbridge.

DONEGAL (EAST) TOWNSHIP.

Solon Z., farmer,	River street, Maytown.

DONEGAL (WEST) TOWNSHIP.

David, farmer,	Elizabethtown.
Franklin K., farmer,	Elizabethtown.
John,	Elizabethtown.
John F., farmer,	Elizabethtown.
Joseph, laborer,	Elizabethtown.
Martin K., laborer,	Elizabethtown.
Phares, laborer,	Elizabethtown.

EARL (WEST) TOWNSHIP.

Augustus, blacksmith,	West Earl.

EPHRATA TOWNSHIP.

Aaron, teamster,	Ephrata.
Daniel, boxmaker,	Akron.
Elam B., farmer,	Lincoln.
G. Geyer, cigar manufacturer,	Ephrata.
Hannah, spinster,	Ephrata.
Hattie, widow,	Ephrata.
Henry, blacksmith,	Akron.
Jacob B., laborer,	
Jacob L., farmer,	
Jacob W., horse dealer,	Ephrata.
J. Harlan, horse dealer,	Ephrata.
John, laborer,	Ephrata.
Levi, retired farmer,	Lincoln.
Priscilla, spinster,	Lincoln.

HEMPFIELD (EAST) TOWNSHIP.

Aaron B., farmer,	Rohrerstown.
Abram, farmer,	Rohrerstown.
Daniel, retired,	East Petersburg.
Daniel H., farmer,	East Petersburg.
David M., laborer,	East Petersburg.
Florence S., dressmaker,	Landisville.
Isaac, laborer,	Rohrerstown.
Israel C., merchant,	(Bamfordville) Landisville.
Jacob, laborer,	Rohrerstown.
Jacob K., laborer,	East Petersburg.
Jeremiah H., farmer,	East Petersburg.
John B., farmer,	East Petersburg.
John S., hotel keeper,	Landisville.
Michael, miller,	Rohrerstown.
Samuel K., cigarmaker,	Landisville.

LAMPETER (EAST) TOWNSHIP.

Aaron D., farmer,	Witmer.
Abraham K., retired farmer,	Greenland.
Abraham L., farmer,	-
Abraham M., farmer,	Witmer.
Abraham S., farmer,	Lancaster.
Adam, farmer,	Lancaster.
Adam L., farmer,	Witmer.
Amos B., farmer,	Witmer.
Barbara R., farmer,	Lancaster.
Benjamin, farmer,	Greenland.
Benjamin, jr., farmer,	Greenland.
Benjamin K., farmer,	Bird-in-Hand.
Benjamin L., farmer,	Lancaster.
Christian D., farmer,	Binkley's Bridge.
Christian N., farmer,	Bird-in-Hand.
Daniel M., farmer,	Fertility.
David, farmer,	Witmer.
David, retired,	Greenland.
David N., farmer,	Bird-in-Hand.
Frank K., thresher,	Lancaster.
Frank J., farmer,	Lancaster.

Harry H., laborer,	Lancaster.
Henry, farmer,	Lancaster.
Henry B., farmer,	Lancaster.
Henry K., farmer,	Lancaster.
Henry M., farmer,	Witmer.
Henry N., retired,	Lancaster.
Henry R., retired,	Lancaster.
Isaac S., farmer,	Witmer.
Israel, farmer,	Witmer.
Jacob, retired,	Greenland.
Jacob L., coachmaker,	·Greenland.
Jacob M., coachmaker,	Fertility.
Jacob R., retired farmer,	Lancaster.
Jacob S., farmer,	Lancaster.
John A., laborer,	Fertility.
John B., laborer,	·
John K., laborer,	Lancaster.
John L., farmer,	Bird-in-Hand.
John L., Rev., retired,	Binkley's Bridge.
John M., wagonmaker,	Fertility.
John N., farmer,	Lancaster.
John S., retired,	Lancaster.
Levi, retired,	Lancaster.
Martin G., retired,	Lancaster.
Moses N., farmer,	Bird-in-Hand.
Peter J., farmer,	Lancaster.
Samuel K., farmer,	Lancaster.

LAMPETER (WEST) TOWNSHIP.

Abraham, retired,	Lancaster.
Adam, farmer,	Lampeter.
Amos M., farmer,	Lampeter.
Christian, farmer,	Fertility.
Daniel M., carpenter,	·
Elmer, laborer,	Lampeter.
John R., laborer,	Willow Street.
William, carpenter,	·

LANCASTER CITY.

Adam G., clerk,	442 North Queen street.
Anna, widow John H.,	217 North Mulberry street.
Annie, widow,	516 West Grant street.
Benjamin F., shoemaker,	508 South Queen street.
Catharine, widow Jacob,	442 North Queen street.
Celinda,	boards at 651 West Orange street.
Charles C.,	boards at 409 East King street.
Charles I., attorney,	24 South Duke street.
Christian D., laborer,	314 Arch alley.
Clayton G.,	boards at 202 East King street.
David B., *Inquirer* Printing Dep't,	320 East Chestnut street.
David B., flour merchant,	202 East King street.
David N., artesian well driller,	Cor. E. King and Church sts.
Eliza, widow Daniel,	516 West Grant street.
Elizabeth A., widow George,	133 East Lemon street.
Elizabeth P., widow Jesse,	24 South Duke street.
Ezra F., steam radiator manufacturer,	532 North Lime street.
Harry, student,	boards at 549 West Chestnut street.
Houston L., salesman,	133 East Lemon street.
Israel L., patentee,	boards at Keystone House.
Jacob D., tobacco packer,	651 West Orange street.
Jacob H., cigarmaker,	512 North Christian street.
James D., managing editor *New Era*,	24 South Duke street.
Jennie, saleswoman,	boards at 524 East Orange street.
John E. Landes, cabinet-maker,	544 East Orange street.
John F., bricklayer,	215 North Mulberry street.
John K., machinist,	532 North Lime street.
John S. Landes, patent-rights,	544 East Orange street.
Joseph, bricklayer,	21 Love Lane.
Kate, widow Philip,	524 East Orange street.
Lemon S., florist,	boards in Lancaster township.
Levi C., machinist,	boards at 409 East King street.
Levi K., machinist,	409 East King street.
Lydia, widow Benjamin,	428 North Duke street.
Martin, laborer,	450 Manor street.
Martin Landes, laborer,	129 Concord alley.
Mary, widow John,	418 Lafayette street.
Michael,	boards at 107 East King street.
Walter,	boards at 516 West Grant street.

LANCASTER TOWNSHIP.

Henry H., laborer,	Lancaster.
John H., laborer,	Lancaster.
Mary A., widow,	Lancaster.

LEACOCK TOWNSHIP.

L. L., farmer,	Intercourse.

LEACOCK UPPER.

Benjamin B., farmer,	Bareville.
Charles A., clerk,	Leacock.
Christian B., farmer,	
Christian R., retired,	Leacock.
David, retired,	Bird-in-Hand.
David F., farmer,	
David N., butcher,	Groff's Store.
Ezra A., farmer,	Binkley's Bridge.
Jacob H., farmer,	Witmer.
John B., laborer,	Bird-in-Hand.
John B., farmer,	
Martin S., retired,	Bareville.
Milton L., farmer,	Leacock.
Nancy, widow,	Binkley's Bridge.
Reuben L., laborer,	Leacock.
Susan, widow John,	Witmer.

MANHEIM BOROUGH.

Josiah H., druggist,	119 North Prussian street.
John, assistant mail carrier,	Cherry street.

MANHEIM TOWNSHIP.

Abraham, laborer,	Oregon.
Andrew R., farmer,	Oregon.
Benjamin B., farmer,	Landis Valley.
Benjamin D., farmer,	Neffsville.
Benjamin L., farmer,	Landis Valley.
Benjamin R., farmer,	Oregon.
Daniel M., farmer,	East Petersburg.
Elam L., farmer,	Landis Valley.

Harry K., farmer,   -   -   -   Landis Valley.
Henry H., farmer,   -   -   -   -   Landis Valley.
Henry L., farmer,   -   -   -   -   Oregon.
Henry S., farmer,   -   -   -   -   Lancaster.
Isaac L., farmer,   -   -   -   -   Oregon.
Isaac M., laborer,   -   -   -   -   -
Isaac R., farmer,   -   -   -   Landis Valley.
Jacob R., farmer,   -   -   -   -   Oregon.
John H. L., farmer,   -   -   -   -
John L., farmer,   -   -   -   -   -   -
John M., farmer,   -   -   -   -   Neffsville.
Levi L., farmer,   -   -   -   -   Neffsville.
Milton H., farmer,   -   -   -   -
Noah L., farmer,   -   -   -   -   Oregon.
Peter R., farmer,   -   -   -   Landis Valley.
Samuel R., farmer,   -   -   -   -   -

MANOR TOWNSHIP.

Amanda Landes, teacher,   -   -   Millersville.
David, retired,   -   -   -   -   Millersville.
David H., miller,   -   -   -   -   Millersville.
Jacob H., retired,   -   -   -   -   Millersville.
John H., Hon., miller,   -   -   -   Millersville.
John S., retired farmer,   -   -   -   Millersville.
John S., laborer,   -   -   -   -   Highville.
Rebecca, widow,   -   -   -   -   Highville.
Tobias H., farmer,   -   -   -   Millersville.

MOUNT JOY BOROUGH.

Abraham B., carriage manufacturer,   -   Barbara street.
Henry H., drover,   -   -   -   West Main street.

MOUNT JOY TOWNSHIP.

Joseph K., laborer,   -   -   -   -   Florin.
J. K., laborer,   -   -   -   Elizabethtown.
Moses, laborer,   -   -   -   -   Elizabethtown.

PENN TOWNSHIP. .

David, farmer,   -   -   -   -   -   Lititz.
Henry R., farmer,   -   -   -   -   -   Lititz.
John K., laborer,   -   -   -   -   Manheim.

PEQUEA TOWNSHIP.

Amos, farmer, ...   New Danville.

RAPHO TOWNSHIP.

Benjamin L., cigar-box manufacturer,   .   Salunga.
Henry farmer, ...   Mount Joy.
Henry M., farmer, ...   Mount Joy.
Jacob, ...   Mount Joy.

STRASBURG BOROUGH.

Daniel K., merchant,   .   .   West Main street.
Joseph,   .   .   Main street, corner Decatur.

WARWICK TOWNSHIP.

David B., ...
H., farmer, ...
H. F., butcher, ...   Rothsville.
Henry, butcher, ...   Rothsville.
Jacob R., cigar manufacturer,   .   .   .   Rothsville.
John, butcher, ...   Rothsville.
John, laborer, ...   Lititz.
Wayne, butcher, ...   Rothsville.

WASHINGTON BOROUGH.

Peter E., laborer,   .   .   .   Water street.

PART VI.

GENERAL ODDS AND ENDS.

MISCELLANEOUS INFORMATION OF A MORE OR LESS INTER-
ESTING CHARACTER CONCERNING THE WORK OF THE
LANDIS FAMILY — AN OLD BIBLE — LATE MARRIAGES
AND DEATHS.

THE name of Landis was known to the French and Germans centuries ago. The French pronounce the word *Lon-da* (or *de*), and the Germans, *Lan-des*—the accent in either instance being on the last syllable. In France the name Landes (londes) was applied long ago to a department in the south-western part of that country, including the Bay of Biscay. Its area is 3,490 square miles. Population in 1876, 303,508. The place is occupied by heaths (landes), whence its name.

Landis is the name of a township of Cumberland county, N. J. Its population is over 7,000.

Landisville is a small post-village in Atlantic county, N. J., on the New Jersey Southern & Vineland Railroad. It has a church. This pretty place was founded by Charles Kline Landis, of Bucks (or Lancaster county, Pa.) descent.

Landisburg, Perry county, Pa., was founded by Abraham Landis, formerly of Lancaster county. It is on Sherman's creek, about fourteen miles north-west of Carlisle. An academy is located there; also, several churches and two tanneries. Population, over 400.

Landis' Store is a post-hamlet of Berks county, this State, about sixteen miles north-east of Reading.

DISCIPLES OF MENNO SIMON.

Rev. Benjamin Landis, one of the first emigrants to this county, was, as previously stated, a Mennonite minister of the

Gospel, and all his descendants to the fifth generation adhered to the Mennonite faith without an exception. Even to this day a majority of the Landis family belong to Menno Simon's church, in which a number have served and are serving as pastors.

Abraham Landis, about 1812,* was one of the first persons to follow Francis Herr in withdrawing from the Old Mennonite church and establishing a new branch called the Reformed Mennonites. On October 10 of that year John Landis was appointed to the ministry and preached his first sermon October 31. He resided at East Lampeter.

A TREASURED BIBLE.

Probably the oldest evidence of the Landis relationship is a Bible now in the possession of Levi S. Reist, of Oregon, this county, whose wife is a great-granddaughter of Benjamin and Anna Landis, once owners of it. Anna's parents (Snavely) brought the sacred volume from Europe. The book was published at Zurich, Switzerland, by Johannes Wolff, in 1596, the numerals MDXCVI being at the beginning of the Old and end of the New Testaments. The family record† contains notices of the children born to Benjamin and Anna Landis prior to the Revolutionary War. The orthography of this old volume seems somewhat odd at this late day, as any German reader will readily notice from a perusal of "Des Alten ond Neiuven Testament." May this rare old Bible witness many more years of service as evidence of the large family of Landis folk.

PUBLIC OFFICERS.

Old records show that Abraham Landis, about 1785, furnished lime for the building of a Court House in Centre Square, Lancaster.

John Landes was one of the first managers of the New Holland & Lancaster turnpike, which was incorporated March 20, 1810.

---

* Evans' History of Lancaster County.
† See Landisville *Vigil*, January 30, 1886.

John Landis, esq., was Supervisor of Conestoga township, in 1817.

Joseph Landis, Marietta, was one of the original contributors to the Zion's church building, that place, in July, 1817.

John Landis was a Justice of Peace in District No. 8 (composed of the townships of Warwick and Elizabeth), August 7, 1832.*

Joseph Landis was County Auditor in 1837.

John Landis was an Alderman of Lancaster city, February 26, 1842.

Emanuel Landis, of Upper Leacock township, was a road Supervisor in 1847.

Benjamin Landis, Upper Leacock, was a Supervisor in 1848; Assessor in 1847 and 1853.

Jacob Landis, Upper Leacock, was Supervisor in 1849.

J. B. Landis, Mount Joy, was one of the borough Councilmen in 1859.

H. H. Landis was one of the incorporators of the Mount Joy Cemetery, which was planned on August 19, 1863.

J. D. Landis, Pequea township, served as Justice of Peace, April, 1874.

David Landis, Adamstown, was a member of the borough Town Council, 1878-9.

PRACTITIONERS IN MEDICINE.

Dr. E. Landis assisted in the organization of the Lancaster City and County Medical Society, at the house of Dr. Eli Parry, on January 14, 1844.

Henry Landis, M. D.,† of Marietta, graduated in 1861, from University of Pennsylvania; was elected a member of the County Medical Society in 1866. Lives now in Reading.

J. R. Landis, M. D., of Elizabethtown, graduated from Jefferson Medical College in 1864; was elected a member of the Medical Society in 1866.

FIRE COMPANIES.

The meeting at which the Washington Fire Company, of Lancaster city, was organized, was held at the house of John

---

*Evans' History of Lancaster County.
† Presiding officer of Ashara Lodge No. 398, A. Y. M., in 1869.

Landis, March 4, 1820, at which 41 persons were present who
were desirous of forming the new company.

Jesse Landis was President of the American Fire Engine
and Hose Company, Lancaster, in 1862.

George B. Landis was President of the Sun Fire Company,
Lancaster, June 1, 1882.

On the night of June 20, 1838, two one-story frame houses
occupied respectively by John Landis and a Mr. Rook, in Lancaster, were destroyed by fire. Landis and his wife, it is said,
were so bewildered that they neglected to carry their two children out, and the record tells us the latter perished in the flames.

RECENT MARRIAGES AND DEATHS.

Among the more recent marriages and deaths not to be
found in Part II. of this work are the following:

On April 19, 1887, Mr. Henry C. Barnhart, formerly of
Mount Joy, was married to Miss Nellie G. Landis, at the residence of the bride's mother, York, this State, by Rev. J. O.
Miller, D. D. Both bride and groom had been employed for
some years in John Baer's Sons' book store, Lancaster.

On November 24, 1887, Miss M. Emma Landis, who taught
school at Locust Grove, West Lampeter township, was joined
in wedlock by Rev. James Y. Mitchell, D. D., of Lancaster,
to Mr. Phares K. Doner, of East Lampeter township.

On December 20, 1887, Mr. Israel S. Sheirk, of Penn township, was wedded at the home of the bride's parents, by Rev.
D. W. Gerhard, to Miss Emma H. Landis, of East Lampeter
township.

On Saturday morning, December 24, 1887, Mr. Abraham
G. Landis, of Voganville, was married by Rev. Charles L.
Fry, at Trinity Lutheran parsonage, Lancaster, to Miss Alice
J. Kraemer, of Voganville, this county.

On the 8th of June, 1887, Jacob L. Landis died in Washington borough, in his 64th year.

A shocking accident on Saturday night, August 20, 1887,
resulted in the death of J. Clayton Landis, a former resident
of Columbia, this county. Landis was making his first trip,
after promotion to brakeman, on a passenger train, in the
employ of the Wilmington & Northern Railroad. At Wilmington, while he went around the rear of his train to place

a switch, he was struck on the head by a shifting engine, and in falling was caught by the rods of the latter, whereby he was horribly mangled. The only part of his body, as reported, remaining whole was the right forearm and wrist. Deceased was 38 years of age, and left a wife and two young children to mourn his loss.

FACTS AND FIGURES.

The painstaking reader who may have been interested sufficiently in this volume to read it through, will notice a number of points, some of which are herewith appended:

The common use made of such surnames as, Benjamin, John, Jacob, Henry, etc., is apparent from the beginning of the family sketches. The word Benjamin occurs 140 times; that of John 312 times; Jacob, 153 times; and Henry, 140 times, including every portion of the book.

The remarkable increase of several members of the family is, also, noticeable. The descendants of "Brick" John Landis, of Lampeter; "Hill" John, of Manheim township, and others, can be enumerated by the hundreds. The decrease of other lineal descendants of the original stock is just as perceptible in a few instances. "So-zu-sauga" John's direct descendants, for instance, number less than a score.

A WISH.

The writer, in conclusion, indulges the hope that, among many others of the large Landis family, he may witness in the year 1917 a grand gathering of descendants of the pioneer settlers on Lancaster county's fertile soil. To properly commemorate the bi-centennial of the arrival of the original stock, there should be such a collection of Landis folk as to make the event, in point of numbers alone, one of much significance. Besides, it would naturally leave in its wake many pleasant memories.

THE END.